MANDY'S
FAVORITE
LOUISIANA RECIPES

MANDY'S

FAVORITE
LOUISIANA RECIPES

formerly entitled
Mirations and Miracles of Mandy

Natalie V. Scott

PELICAN PUBLISHING COMPANY
GRETNA 2003

First Pelican edition, 1978
Second printing, 1980
Third printing, 1983
Fourth printing, 1985
Fifth printing, 1987
Sixth printing, 1988
Seventh printing, 1995
Eighth printing, 1998
Ninth printing, 2003

Printed in the United States of America
Published by Pelican Publishing Company, Inc.
1000 Burmaster Street, Gretna, Louisiana 70053

Cover illustration from "Annie" by
Elizabeth O'Neill Verner. Mrs. Verner's
eye and hand have taught four genera-
tions to see, to love, and to preserve the
heritage of Charleston, South Carolina.

Mirations and Miracles of Mandy

Some Favorite Louisiana Recipes

"MY madam say she writin' mah cookin' down. Lawdy, put me frontin' a cookin' stove, an' I don't needs no prescription", says Mandy.

Mandy, of course, is a composite.

My own Mandy's name is Pearl. Bless her earnest face, and her soft voice, and her good brown eyes,—and bless particularly that vital sixth culinary sense, which creates delectable miracles of food without 'no prescription!'

There are the Mandys of all my friends,—Mammy Lou, and Phrosine, and Tante Celeste, Venida, Felicie, Mande, Titine, Elvy, Mona, Relie. It is said that the witch doctors of North Africa have a mastery of mental telepathy. These Mandys, too, have some such subtle sense. They become miraculously aware of this way of dealing with a vegetable, that way of concocting a soup. They have culinary tentacles of the spirit always aquiver to appropriate each good new idea.

New Orleans exposes them to many. We have among us exponents of many culinary learnings; the herbs of France, and its sauces; the oil and the garlic of Spain; the pastes of Italy; the meal and chili of Mexico; hot-breads from South Carolina and Virginia; pot pies from Germany and New England; chefs d'oeuvres, creations of our own master restaurateurs, unexcelled as they are. Somehow, mysteriously, the Mandys acquire them, only to let them reappear slightly altered and marked with the stamp of their own cult, which is the stamp of inspiration.

In the various cuisines of which they are the muses, mysterious rites go on, heritage of many countries, heritage of many years. I have peeped here, watched there, borrowed and begged, and doubtless, inadvertently stolen, to offer in these scant pages a few of these local treasures.

Above all, I have tried to keep to the simple and practical and the inexpensive, to avoid the extravagant. In the old days, when Mandy had her ranks of helpers and lavish living was the rule, she evolved intricacies and complexities and extravagancies. A hundred oysters, a dozen eggs, a quart of cream, were simple items in any recipe (we call them receipts, by the way!). But Mandy, whose resources surmount her regrets, has adapted herself. She still has the rich rash 'plat' for guests;

but she has, too, the simple, economical, and still delicious dishes that make a feast of the family dinner. This is as it should be. Our relish of her efforts spurs the inspiration, for we, who are both French and Southern, have the conviction that good eating is one of the legitimate joys of life.

Herbs are of her fundamentals. Once, far away from my 'Mandy', I looked into the kitchen of the quaint old Inn of Guillaume le Conquerant, at Dives-Cabourg. It dates back to 1400 or so, always in the same family. There, on the great table, a whole slab of a giant tree, before the mammoth fireplace, under ancient rafters, were little piles of chopped herbs arranged neatly in a row; thyme, and parsley, bay leaf, shallot tops. Homesickness suddenly clenched my heart in its hand; those homely little heaps were movingly familiar! The 'repairin' knife as Mandy calls it, comes into constant play, mincing the herbs to delicate fineness.

She likes her garlic: do not distrust it,—with proper restraint, it gives a matchless 'gout'. Some people find that simply rubbing it on the dish gives sufficient flavor to salads. Thyme must be used sparingly, or it will subdue everything else. Finely chopped green peppers play an important role, with the parsley, shallot (small green onion) tops, bay leaf, sage, onion, and garlic,—as Africa inherits from William's Normandy, at the discretion of our Mandy.

Dear Mandys. They are integrally of our life, part of its suavity. They trick us, harass us and serve us; understand us amazingly, and love us. And we,—we scold them, distrust them, rely on them, take care of them, love them. Wanting a more worthy token, I offer them this little tribute, with, fittingly, echoes of their homely wisdom and reflections of their homely but true art.

"good talkin' mought mek happy comp'ny; but good eatin' sure do."

"rough talk turn smoov in de mouf, ef yo' got a tasty somep'n ter pop inter it."

OYSTER COCKTAIL-SAUCE ANTIBES

Your guests will probably like ½-dozen oysters each,—and certainly this sauce: to each 1 tablespoon of tomato catsup, 1 teaspoon of Worcestershire sauce, juice of ½ a lemon, 1 drop of tabasco, salt, and pepper. A dash of horseradish with this, if you wish. A piece of celery heart makes for looks as well as taste.

CRAB-MEAT COCKTAIL, SAUCE PASS CHRISTIAN

Use white crab-meat only, carefully picked. A little celery may be chopped up with it.

1 cup of mayonnaise
1 tablespoon of tomato catsup
1 teaspoon of anchovy paste
1 tablespoon of Worcestershire
Salt, pepper, paprika

Dissolve the anchovy paste in the Worcestershire sauce. Vinegar may be used instead.
Mix the ingredients together. Have them well chilled, and the crab-meat as well. Pour the mixture over the crab-meat and garnish it with short celery stalks.
This goes as happily with shrimp cocktail.

SHRIMP COCKTAIL SAUCE CREOLE

1 tablespoon of Worcestershire sauce
1 cup of tomato catsup
1 tablespoon of horseradish
1 tablespoon of vinegar
2 tablespoons of lemon juice
3 drops of tabasco
2 teaspoons of Creole mustard
Salt.
Chill well

This will go for crab-meat, too.

SARDINE COCKTAIL

Sardines
Celery
Cocktail Sauce

Prepare crisp toast, in nice shapes. Cut the celery and sardines separately, not too small. Then, a layer of celery on the toast, then a layer of sardines, celery again, and cocktail sauce over all.

COCKTAIL SAUCE CELESTE

1 cup of mayonnaise
2 tablespoons of chili sauce, and add tarragon vinegar to please your taste.

HORS D'OEUVRES VIENNE

"grace kin raise de low up high,—en' fixin is de grace o' food."

½ lb. of small Vienna sausage
½ loaf of bread
Butter

Slice fresh bread very thin. Butter it sparely, and wrap it in a very damp napkin letting it remain for an hour. Skin the sausages and slice them lengthwise. Roll a slice of bread around each slice of sausage, and hold it in place with a piece of toothpick. Brown in a quick oven and serve at top heat.
They are very good baked in biscuit dough. Anchovies may be similarly treated.

CHILLED TOMATOES

Tomatoes
Eggs
Mayonnaise
Celery
Olives, anchovies, capers
Anchovy paste

Hollow the tomatoes. Chop up the hard boiled egg, olives, anchovies, celery, and capers, and mix them with the mayonnaise. Fill the tomatoes with the mixture.

Mix a little anchovy paste with mayonnaise, and put some on top of each of the tomatoes. Put this in the frigidaire, or in a freezer packed with ice.

EGGS BERNARD

Eggs
Sliced boiled ham
Bouillon
Gelatine, parsley

Poach the eggs. Do not let them cook too much. Put each in a mold, 'face' down, lay a thin slice of ham over it.

Dissolve the gelatine and add to the bouillon enough to congeal it, and pour it over the eggs. Set it to harden. Present it garnished with lettuce and parsley.

JELLIED HAM

2 cups of boiled ham
1 cup of cream
2 teaspoons of mustard
4 tablespoons of mayonnaise
2 tablespoons of gelatine
½ cup of cold water
1 cup of horseradish

Mince the ham very finely and mix it with the horseradish and the mustard.

Whip the cream and add it to the mayonnaise. Soak the gelatine a bit in cold water, dissolve it in hot water. When it has cooked a little, strain it into the cream.

Put it to cool ¼ of an hour, then add the ham. Pour in a mold, pack it with ice, and let it stand several hours.

STUFFED CELERY

N. Y. Cream Cheese
Celery
Raisins, stuffed olives
Salt, pepper, paprika

Save the tenderest stalks to be stuffed. Chop up the root and other stalks and stuffed olives. Mash the mixture up with the cream cheese, add a few chopped raisins and a pinch of salt; a little white pepper. Shave down the ends of the celery and dip them in paprika then fill them with the paste. It looks as well as it tastes.

CELERY RUSSE

The tender stalks of celery filled with caviar, sprinkled lightly with lemon juice and a little powdered yolk of eggs, is delicious, a 'bon bouche' with cocktails (alcoholic!).

TOMATOES RIS-DE-VEAU

1 lb. of sweetbreads
Tomatoes
Mayonnaise
Caviar

Parboil the sweetbreads for ½ an hour in salt water, let them cool, pull them apart and peel them. Chop them up finely and mix them with mayonnaise. Have the tomatoes skinned and chilled, and set in a nest of shredded lettuce. Put the sweetbread mixture on top of each, then a touch of mayonnaise. A little caviar to round off the delicacy.

CANAPÉ D'ANCHOIS

"him is in a high seat don' need no horn ter tell erbout it." In other words, anchovies need little assistance to make an impression.

1 tablespoon of mayonnaise
2 tablespoons of anchovy paste
½ teaspoon of Worcestershire
Hard boiled eggs
Tabasco, ½ lemon

The mayonnaise and paste stirred well together, Worcestershire, tabasco, and juice of the lemon. Mix them well, and spread very thinly on thin crisp buttered toast. Have the white and yolk finely chopped, separately, and garnish the toast with it.

BROILED OLIVES

Stuffed Olives
Bacon

Wrap large stuffed olives each in ½ slice of bacon, fastened with a piece of toothpick. Broil them and drain them on butcher's paper.

CRAB CANAPÉ LORENZO

"whar-erbout count much as whur: de crab on'y go backwa'd in de water, but he go mo' ways den one on de table."

The same recipe which you will discover for stuffed crabs (page 26) is the beginning of a most effective canapé. Add some cheese sauce to this 'stuffing,' smooth it thickly over toast, and cross 2 anchovies on top. Run this in the oven a few minutes. Take it out, and scatter a mixture of finely grated cheese with very finely crumbled (and few!) bread crumbs, over the top; a dab of butter here and there, and back into the oven for browning. Garnished with parsley and grated lemon, it is chic.

COLD CHICKEN CANAPÉ

Breast of chicken
Potatoes
Eggs
Celery, ripe olive, pimento
Mayonnaise

Boil the potatoes and the eggs. Chop them up with all the other ingredients and mix them with the mayonnaise. Serve on crisp buttered toast.

"sta'tin on de wrong foot ain' nevah win, de race: a good dinnah don' git ncwhah ef de soup ain' right."

"meny ez dey got cooks in de kitchens, da's how many ways you kin ster up a gumbo."

Mandy knows her gumbos,—a good cook can make as many variations of gumbo as a jazz composer can of a Bach theme. But the theme is there, for the gumbo as for the music. Okra or filé (which is mysterious for ground dried sassafras leaves) is part of it. If the market man has no fresh okra, the grocer will oblige with some in cans. Filé is usually back on the shelf somewhere, too. If not, order it out of New Orleans.

A roux of flour and lard is the initial step, followed by an orgy of seasoning ad lib. —thyme, bay leaf, peppers, onions, green onion top, parsley, celery, chopped and intermingled. A bit of tabasco. Chicken, oysters, crabs, or shrimp, may be used separately or together. There, again, the can may do its bit. With all except the oysters, a piece of ham-bone, or a bit of veal-stew should play a part.

Rice is its Siamese twin, artificially joined: it may be offered separately, after the gumbo is served. It may adopt the elegance of being served in a mold.

"full o' grace kin be cantanc'ous: Okra good 'nough, but sho' turn black fo' yo' in de wrong pot."

True: it demands porcelain,—otherwise it goes into a dark rage, turns quite black and impossible.

OYSTER GUMBO FILÉ

1 scant tablespoon of lard
2 tablespoons of flour
2 dozen (or more) oysters

Chopped onion, green onion top, thyme, bay leaves, parsley, salt, pepper, drops of tabasco

1 tablespoon of filé
Rice

Brown the flour and lard: a few drops of water deflect the peril of burning. Add seasonings and let simmer. To the liquor of the oysters add water till there is about 3 quarts of liquid in all. Abandon all to the mercy of a moderate fire for half an hour. About fifteen minutes before the dinner hour, add oysters and chopped parsley. When ready to serve, remove from the stove, drop in the filé and stir with vim. Serve with rice,— and be proud!

CRAB OKRA GUMBO

1 tablespoon of lard
1 dozen crabs
1 piece of ham, or veal stew, or both
1 small can of tomatoes (or 6 fresh ones)
1 quart of okra

Chopped onion, green onion top, thyme, bay leaves, parsley, a leek, salt, pepper, drops of tabasco
Rice

Cut the okra in small pieces (after it has been cleaned and stemmed). Scald the crabs, pull off the legs, and clean the crabs well; then quarter them, saving the quartered pieces and the claws for use in the gumbo. Fry the okra in the lard with the ham and veal stew (if used). Add 2 quarts of water and the crabs and resume the gentle cooking, for about an hour. **Note:** Flour is usually not used in an okra gumbo.

You may use fewer crabs, and use shrimp with them, if you like.

Lake shrimp may substitute for their kindred in either of the above recipes. They are a bit more effective with okra than with filé, but rate very high in both recipes.

They must be boiled in very highly seasoned water,—garlic, salt, pepper, cloves, thyme, bay leaves, and the rest—to give them a taste. Of course, they are peeled before being put in the gumbo. The water in which they are boiled may be strained and used in the gumbo very advantageously. Oyster water in a shrimp gumbo is another step in the right direction.

GUMBO Z'HERBES

"a big man tote a heavy load, an a good gumbo kin mos' ca'ry a dinnah."

Truly the queen of all Gumbos is gumbo z'herbes. It can be nearly as complex as the human form—and likewise as divine—when Mandy is in a fury of creation. But even we ordinary mortals can achieve a culinary masterpiece by following the general directions given below, with variations according to discretion, necessity, or inspiration.

2 tablespoons of lard
2 tablespoons of flour
1 bunch each of spinach, mustard greens, green cabbage, beet tops, roquette, water cress, radishes
Chopped onion, parsley, thyme, bay leaf, green onion top, salt, pepper, red pepper pod, or drop of tabasco.
Bacon strip, veal or pork brisket, or ham bone

As many kinds of greens as possible: you can do without any one or two or so,—but not without all! Wash well the greens, put in hot water and boil well. Drain off the water and save it.

Fry the meat in 1 tablespoon of lard, chopping up, the while, the greens with the onion and seasoning.

Take out the meat and fry the greens, stirring solicitously, for they would rather burn than not.

When they are well fried, add the flour, take a breath, and stir some more. Season well.

Add the meat and the treasured water of the boiled greens; leave all to simmer for an hour or so.

One last rite and you will have earned the joy you will have in your creation,— stir in 1 tablespoon of flour dissolved in cold water. It has the magic effect on greens of making them melt in your mouth like cream.

"ain't-none kin pa'alyze yo': bes' fix yo' min' on I-got."

Gumbos may seem alarmingly complex. Take heart,—with judgment ingredients may be omitted and yet a worthy dish appear. Seasonings may be less—a little!—and, risking the charge of sacrilege, I say even without the veal or ham touch, a pleasing product be achieved.

CRAB GUMBO A L'ANGLAIS

This is a gumbo which Mandy scorns for its simplicity and considers an affront to its name, because it has neither okra, nor filé, nor flour. But—out of her earshot—it can be recommended.

1 tablespoon of lard
1 pound of boiled shrimp
1 dozen crabs (the meat)
Hambone, or bacon, or veal stew.
Garlic, thyme, bay leaf, a large onion, parsley, salt, pepper, drops of tabasco

Chop up the onions and seasoning and brown the lot in a frying-pan with a tablespoon of lard. When it is properly golden, add the crab meat and shrimp, and the ham-bone, and let them brown. Then add a quart of water and boil moderately for half an hour.

GOLD TIP GUMBO

"some sez eben de debble's tail got a gold tip."

This was Mandy's comment on a memorable occasion. A colored porter friend of hers brought a gumbo back from the West, whence she expected no culinary excellence. He made her try it and, on her conscience as an artist she had to admit it was good.

1 hen (not too elderly)
2 Irish potatoes
2 tablespoons of rice
½ quart of tomatoes
½ quart of okra
1 dozen macaroni sticks
Ham bone, or slice, and bacon
Thyme, bay leaf, garlic, onion, parsley, drops of tabasco, and of Worcestershire,
Salt, pepper
1 gallon of water

Cut the hen and fry to a golden brown. Then let it boil slowly one hour in a gallon of water. Take it out, chop the meat fine and put it back in the pot.

Fry the bacon, or ham, with the onion, and add it, drippings and all, with all the other ingredients, to the chicken. (The macaroni should be broken in short lengths—for all but native born Italians!) Season, and let it simmer moderately for an hour.

soups {11}

CREAM OF CRAB SOUP

1 tablespoon of flour
2 tablespoons of butter
2 quarts of milk
1 pint of crab meat
½ onion
½ pint whipping cream
Chopped parsley, celery, onion salt, salt, white pepper

Cream the butter and flour together. Put the milk in a double boiler and add the creamed butter and flour to it, then the onion, and the seasoning at your palate's discretion.

Let it all cook calmly till the soup thickens a little, then add the crab-meat. Serve with dabs of whipped cream. Your reputation as a hostess is assured.

OYSTER SOUP LOUISIANE

"oyster soup, it's lak ev'ything else: times it laks fixin's, times it don't."

1 quart of oysters
1 quart of milk
1 tablespoon of butter
Salt, white pepper, onion salt, chopped parsley

Put the oyster liquor in one saucepan the milk in another. To the juice add the seasoning, including the parsley. Let the two saucepans come to the boiling-point, —so far and no farther.

Add the liquor to the milk, stirring faithfully. Add the butter, then put the oysters in gradually. The law about oysters is that they must not boil: a safety-first measure is to put the milk in a double-boiler. When the oysters puff and the edges crinkle, serve at once.

OYSTER SOUP A MIRACLE

1 quart of oysters
1 pint of water
1 tablespoon of butter
1 tablespoon of flour
Chopped parsley, green onion top, red pepper, brown onion juice

Brown the butter and flour, with the usual precaution against burning. Add the seasoning. Pour in the oyster liquor and additional water, about a pint, turn the fire low, and let simmering take its course for half an hour.

Add oysters and chopped parsley, and additional seasonings.

When the oysters begin to get bloated, the operation is complete and you have a soup to be proud of.

TURTLE SOUP DE FAMILLE

"comp'ny don' reckon de cos'; but in de fam'ly how much stan' nex' to how good."

In this composition, the humble red bean serves and makes a dish quite like and almost as good as that achieved by the lordly turtle.

(Note: Early childhood recollection,— I was allowed to stop in a little country store to buy candy. As I stood there, a little picaninny marched in directly up to the counter, looked up over it with wide white-accented eyes and reeled off, "Quartee-red-beans, quartee-rice-lagniappe-please-suh." 'Quartee' is half a nickle; 'lagniappe' is a 'present' habitually given with purchases once,—a custom that has lapsed!)

½ pint of red beans
Water
1 tablespoon of flour
1 tablespoon of butter
Onion, lemon, salt, pepper, cayenne, garlic, tabasco
1 cup of grape juice, cooking wine, or sherry flavoring.
2 hard-boiled eggs

Boil the beans until they are tender, then mash them through a sieve. Save the water in which they were boiled. Brown the onion and the flour in the butter, and add this, with the beans, to the water, about 1½ quarts. Peel the lemon and add it. Season highly, and let it simmer tranquilly for an hour. Add the sherry flavoring, or grape juice, or wine, if you are lucky enough to have some.

Just before serving, add chopped hard-boiled eggs, or better still, mock turtle eggs.

CRAB SOUP

1 doz. crabs
1 heaping tablespoon of butter
1 scant tablespoon of flour
1 onion, piece of celery, green onion top, thyme, parsley, salt, pepper, tabasco
2 cups of water
3 cups of boiled milk

Boil and pick crabs, and the worst is over.

Brown the flour and butter together with the onion; add the crab meat, herbs, seasonings, and the water, and let it all simmer together for half an hour. When ready to serve, add the boiled milk.

TURTLE SOUP

"yas'm; things is diff'ent how yo' take 'em: turtle don't git nowhar in a race, but come to soup, he go long ways."

2 lbs. of turtle meat.
2 tablespoons of flour
1 tablespoon of lard
1 small piece of ham
1 piece of lemon
Chopped onions, cloves, garlic, bay leaf, thyme, parsley, salt, pepper

Cut the ham in bits; mash herbs and seasonings with it, and put them aside to bide their time.

Boil the turtle meat fifteen minutes; take it off, and save the stock. Chop up the meat.

Brown the onions in the lard; add the turtle meat and let it brown well. Then add the ham and seasoning, stirring conscientiously. Then comes the flour, always with stirring.

Add the stock at this point, and more water, 2½ to 3 quarts, with salt and various peppers, and also the lemon, chopped very fine. Put in a double boiler for an hour or so, stirring at frequent intervals.

Boil the turtle eggs, chop them fine, and add to the soup when it is ready to serve.

One may still further and pleasantly complicate this delight by adding 2 tomatoes, and some sherry flavoring, or that miracle, a glass of Madeira, or cooking wine, or grape juice. The tomatoes must be skinned and scalded, and chopped, then added to the turtle meat as it browns. The Madeira, or its alternative, is the final touch, added just when the treat is ready to be served.

The eggless turtle need not discourage you. The more dependable hen comes to your rescue.

See Mock Turtle Eggs, toward the end of this chapter.

CONSOMME SUPREME

1 lb. of beef
1 chicken
Water
1 tablespoon of butter
Chopped ham, onions, carrots, bay leaf, thyme, parsley, celery, salt, pepper, tabasco

Dice the chicken and beef, immerse them in cold water and leave them to heat very, very slowly for 3 or 4 hours.

Chop up the ham, onions, and carrots, cook them in the butter, and add them

to the stock. Chop the celery and herbs, and add them, with seasoning, leaving all to the ministration of a moderate heat, for an hour. Then strain, cool, and skim off the grease.

Now add the following: whites of 2 eggs, lightly beaten; their shells; chopped celery and seasoning; juice of ½ a lemon; 2 tablespoons of cold water. Boil for five minutes. Strain, and season. It may now cool; and you can heat it again when your guests, or your invalid friend, desire.

OX-TAIL SOUP

Ox-tail
Bits of ham
2 tablespoons of butter (or lard)
2 quarts of stock (or water)
4 tablespoons of flour
Carrots, celery, parsley, onions, turnip, cayenne, salt, pepper, sherry flavoring (wine, or grape juice)
1 teaspoon of lemon juice
Yolks of hard-boiled eggs

The ham and the ox-tail start out separately, but soon get together. Cut the ox-tail in short lengths; dredge with flour, and fry in butter till it is an even brown.

The bits of ham, chopped with onions, carrots, turnip, celery, parsley, take their place in another saucepan, to be sautés with butter till pleasantly brown. Then add the flour and brown once more.

Then add the stock (or boiling water) and let it boil 40 minutes. Add salt, pepper, cayenne etc. Pour the stock over the ox-tail.

The sherry flavoring, lemon juice, and egg, are not vital, but are highly recommended. Once added, you may present this soup as turtle soup without fear of successful contradiction.

MILKLESS POTATO SOUP

6 Irish potatoes
1 large tablespoon of butter
1 scant tablespoon of flour
2 yolks of eggs
Celery, parsley, onion juice, thyme
6 cups of water

Boil the potatoes, and press them through a colander, then mash them thoroughly. Add 6 cups of water.

Brown the flour in the butter and add the potatoes and water with the chopped celery, parsley, thyme, salt, white pepper. Beat in two egg yolks just before serving. You will never miss the cow.

CREAM OF ONION SOUP

4 onions
1 tablespoon of butter
½ cup of flour
1 pint of water
3 large potatoes
1 quart of milk
Parsley, salt, celery salt, white pepper

Skin the onions and brown them in butter.

Add the flour, stirring vigilantly, until brown.

Stir in the water, adding it slowly to avoid the catastrophe of glue-like lumps. Boil and mash the potatoes, and stir them into a quart of boiling milk, and here again, beware of lumps. Add the fried onions, season discreetly, and boil for 5 minutes. And you have a rich hygienic soup. It is a happy thought to pour it over thin strips of toast.

ONION SOUP PAYSAN

"ev'ything got its 'dat's all'; dis hyah onion soup come mighty near to be it fo' a dinnah."

6 large onions (for 6 persons)
Olive oil
Grated Parmesan cheese
Sliced imported Swiss cheese
7 cups of water
Salt, pepper, cayenne, chopped parsley
Toast

Skin the onions and slice them. (It saves your tears, if you perform this operation under water.) Put the sliced onions in a saucepan with just enough olive oil to keep them from burning. Let them cook until brown, and then cook some more, till they are nearly black and another minute would burn them. Stir at intervals. It needs about 20 minutes. Have the water boiling in a pot. Put the fried onions in and let them boil 20 minutes. 2 minutes before removing, add the sliced Swiss cheese, about 12 thin slices.

Have plates ready with squares of thin toast heaped with grated Parmesan cheese. Pour the soup over the cheese and toast, and serve at once. You will think you are in the Restaurant des Peres Tranquils in Paris, and the rest of the dinner won't matter.

SPINACH SOUP

1 pint boiled spinach
2 heaping tablespoons of butter
2 quarts of stock (or oyster liquor)
1 teaspoon of sugar
Nutmeg, salt, pepper, onion salt

Boil the spinach, chop, and beat it well. Sprinkle it with nutmeg, add salt and pepper, and onion salt, and cook in a tablespoon of butter for about ten minutes. Add the stock, or oyster liquor, and just let it boil, a moment only. Take it off, strain it, and set it back on the fire till it comes to a boil again. Then add a tablespoon of butter and the sugar. It is good for your taste and your health.

GROUND ARTICHOKE SOUP

1 lb. of ground (Jerusalem) artichokes
1 scant tablespoon of butter
1 quart of sweet milk
1 egg
¼ pint of cream
Salt, white pepper, onion juice, chopped celery

Peel and boil the artichokes, and pass them through a colander. Add the milk, butter and seasonings, and let them stew peacefully, until the mixture thickens. Beat the egg and cream together and pour the soup over them. A dab of whipped cream on each plate is a pleasant touch. Oh, delicious!

RICH OYSTER SOUP

2 doz. oysters
Small stalk of celery
2 tablespoons of butter
2 tablespoons of flour
1 quart of milk
Salt, white pepper, chopped parsley

Chop up the celery, cover it with water (about 1 pint) and boil it gently for half an hour or so. Wash the oysters and stew them for five minutes. Take them out, chop them up, and back with them again into the liquor in which they were boiled. Things are coming on. Unite the boiled celery and oysters, together with a quart of milk. Mix the flour and butter together and put it with the rest to cook ten minutes or more. Put in the chopped parsley and seasoning, and you have a wonderful soup.

Elegance requires that it be strained before serving; but the old country style of leaving in all ingredients has its good points.

CRAYFISH BISQUE

"crayfish bisque it's lak a good madam: yo' give it good wu'k, it gonna give yo' good pay."

The vital ingredients are time and patience. There are two elements of a crayfish bisque, besides: the HEADS, with their stuffing, and the STOCK. United in a grand finale, they are a joy to the gourmet.

4 doz. (or more) crayfish
¾ cup of bread (or 4 sodacrackers)
1 tablespoon of butter
1 tablespoon of flour
1 egg
1 onion, herbs, parsley, green onion, salt, white pepper

STUFFED HEADS

Soak the crayfish well in a strong brine for 1 hour. Then wash them well in several waters and even scrub them with a brush—they are not tidy beasts! Boil them and save the water for the stock.

Pick the crayfish, clean the heads and save them, and save all the meat from the bodies.

Wet the bread (or crackers) then squeeze them well. Chop up the meat and add it to the bread.

The flour and butter get together now: they must be browned, then the seasoning added, the chopped green onions, herbs, and all; then, after a moment or two, the crayfish meat whereupon everything must simmer together a few minutes.

Take it off and put it in a bowl, add an egg, mixing it in well. Fill the heads with the mixture, sprinkle them with flour, and fry them a few minutes with a little butter.

STOCK

Water from boiled crayfish
3 tablespoons of flour
2 tablespoons of butter
1 carrot, piece of celery, herbs, parsley, salt, pepper

Brown the butter and flour, add the seasoning, then the water, and let it boil slowly. Just before serving, add the heads. Taste, and your labor is rewarded.

—or—

STOCK

Water from boiled crayfish
Soup brisket
2 onions, 2 carrots
3 tablespoons of flour
2 tablespoons of butter
Chopped parsley, salt, pepper

Let the brisket boil slowly several hours in the water from the boiled crayfish. Add onions and carrots. Brown butter and flour together; pour the butter into it, and add fried crayfish heads.

—or—

STOCK

Water from boiled crayfish
Picked meat and shells of 2 doz. crayfish
1 cup of rice
2 tablespoons of butter
1 quart of oyster liquor
1 onion, carrot, piece of celery, herbs, salt, pepper

Ply your knife into the herbs, onion, carrot, garlic, and chop them fine. Put them with the picked meat and the crayfish shells and a cup of rice, and let the fire at it till it thickens. Take it off, mash the meat and shells as much as possible, and strain. Add the butter and oyster liquor, season well with black and white and red pepper, and salt. Let it come to boil, then serve,—with the knowledge that culinary art can go no further.

SPLIT PEA SOUP

1 cup of split peas (green or yellow)
2 quarts of water
1 quart of milk
1 tablespoon of butter
1 tablespoon of flour
1 strip of bacon (or ham, or sausage)
½ an onion, salt, pepper, red pepper pod

Split peas are a hard proposition: it needs several hours' soaking to bring them to a state of grace. After that, boil them with the bacon, ham, or sausage, and seasoning until they are quite soft, then press them through a colander. Make a roux of the flour and butter, add the peas with the milk and water. Cow peas, sometimes known by their alias of lentils, may serve instead of peas.

CHICKEN SOUP A L'AMANDE

3 cups of chicken stock
1 pint of milk
½ pint of cream
½ cup of blanched almonds
1 tablespoon of butter
1 tablespoon of flour
Pepper, salt, onion juice, bay leaves

Add the milk and seasonings to the chicken stock, and some of the almonds,

soups

well-ground. Stir melted butter into a little flour and add this to the liquid.

It must come to the boiling point—so far and no farther.

Serve it with whipped cream on top of each plate, with ground almonds sprinkled over the cream. It is the top of elegance and of, literally, good taste.

BOUILLON DE LEGUME

1 large can of tomatoes
1 large stalk of celery
Carrots, onion, parsley, green pepper, bay leaf, salt, pepper, onion juice
Sherry flavoring

This is a sweet simplicity of a soup. Chop up the celery, peppers, onion, parsley, etc. Put the tomatoes in a saucepan, adding a pint (or more) of water. Add the chopped ingredients, and let it all boil with restraint a half hour.

Strain. Add sherry flavoring, salt, onion juice, pepper. Serve piping hot, or add gelatin, cool, and serve in bouillon cups,—depending on the thermometer.

Clear with white of egg before adding gelatine.

SOUP STOCK

3 lbs. of soup brisket
3 quarts of water
1 soup bunch with carrot, celery, onion, leek, et cet.
1 potato
3 tomatoes (or 1 small can)
Salt, pepper, thyme, bay leaf, parsley

Have the water boiling. Salt generously and add the brisket to it, as well as any other odds and ends of meat,—luck is with you if you have some giblets of fowls available.

Chop up the soup bunch, tomatoes, potato, and when the bubbling is going merrily, put them in. Let it boil away for about three hours, and you have a goldmine, on which you can draw for a base for all sorts of rich soups,—and it will even stand the necessary dilution when an unexpected guest comes in!

SOUP SUBSIDIARIES

"red look mo' so, 'longside o' yaller; de same way, a tasty li'l some'p'n kin put mo' life in a soup."

Bread can be versatile in abetting a soup. Little cubes of it, buttered and browned, make delicious 'croutons' to drop in. It may be shaped like almonds for the same use.

Toast looks attractive cut in triangles, thin and crisp, or in thin strips. Mandy is likely to brown her bread a little first, then take it out, dip it lightly in melted butter, and back with it into the oven, where it turns beautifully golden. It is a bit extravagant as a process, but effective.

Small square saltines lightly buttered and crisped are delicious; but plain soda crackers, similarly toasted, are better with cream soups. A little grated cheese adds grace to toasted bread and to crackers. It calls for a dash of cayenne, and Mandy sometimes puts paprika.

CUSTARD BITS

Beat up 2 eggs and add to them 2 tablespoons of milk, with a pinch of salt. Pour it into a buttered cup, set in a pan of hot water, and cook in a very slow oven until firm: it will not be long. Take it out of the cup, and slice it, or cut into shapes with a vegetable cutter. It gives character to consomme.

CRACKER BALLS

Beat two eggs, and add salt and pepper, and a tablespoon of butter to them. Crush 6 crackers with the rolling pin and pass them through a sifter, and add them to the eggs. Sculp them into little balls and put in the soup just before it appears on the table.

MOCK TURTLE EGGS

Mash the yolks of hard-boiled eggs (hen's) with a little butter. Add a beaten raw egg, and you have a material which as clever cook you sculp to the shape of turtle eggs. Drop them for a brief 2 minutes into boiling water. Not even a turtle could distinguish them from her bona fide eggs. A little cayenne pepper is a happy thought mixed with them.

After they are shaped, they may be rolled in flour and sauté in butter instead of being dropped in the boiling water.

MARROW BALLS

Soak a slice of bread, then squeeze it, Brown it in a pan with a ½-cup of marrow melt. Take it off and add an egg and some seasoning. Shape it into balls, and drop them into the soup just a few minutes before serving it. Delicious!

EGG-BALLS WITH MATZOS

2 eggs
1 tablespoon of butter
1 cup of Matzos flour
Salt

Beat the yolks of the eggs energetically with the butter. Sift the Matzos and stir it in. Lastly, beat up the whites and add them, with a pinch of salt. Mold like balls, and they will be a great addition to your consomme.

NOODLES

"'sto' made come mo' easy, mebbe; but home-made come mo' good."

One egg, some flour, and a bit of salt are all the ingredients. Beat up the egg, add a pinch of salt, and work in the flour, as much as the egg will take. Flour the bread board, and roll out your 'dough' to its uttermost of thinness. Set it aside on a thin piece of clean paper and let it stand for at least 20 minutes.

It can be cut in fancy shapes as the final step. Or,—the paper itself may be rolled into a long cylinder, like a jelly roll, dough and all; but, take care, the layers of dough must not stick. Then slice thin across this cylinder; shake the layers lightly till they fall apart and then spread the strips to dry thoroughly. They will last for months in tight receptacles.

"mighty high tempah don' bow low ter good eatin'."

EGGS CREOLE

1 doz. hard-boiled eggs
1 large can of tomatoes
1 cup of chopped celery
1 cup of chopped green peppers
1 small can of mushrooms
2 good tablespoons of flour
1 heaping tablespoon of butter
1 onion, salt, black pepper, red, Worcestershire sauce
1 cup of white sauce

Chop the whites of the eggs, and mash the yolks. Strain the tomatoes, for only the juice is going to play a part in this. Now action begins:

The onion, chopped very fine, must fry a little. Next come the peppers, with the flour, and a thorough simmering till they are done,— but not brown. Put in the tomato juice and mushrooms, with salt, and pepper, and do not spare the Worcestershire.

When all of this is well cooked, add the white sauce, and bring out your ramekins. Put the mixture in, sprinkle with cracker-crumbs, dab butter about, and brown them in the oven. Serve hot and proudly.

EGGS AU BEURRE NOIR

Eggs
Butter
Vinegar
Salt, pepper

Put some butter in a saucepan: this butter is to be sauce, so judge the quantity according to the number of eggs you intend to use. Let the butter cook till it is black, and break your eggs in it, one by one, keeping them whole. Salt them, and pepper them, and let them cook for five minutes. Then slip them off onto a serving platter, with all neatness and despatch, and pour the butter over them. Just a moment,—into the still hot saucepan put a good tablespoon of vinegar, and then pour it over the eggs. They are luscious morsels. It is nice to cook them in individual shirring dishes and serve them so.

EGGS FLORENTINE

Eggs
Spinach
Cream sauce
Salt, pepper

These are shirred with spinach,—thus: Butter the shirrer and line it with finely ground cracker or bread crumbs. Break the egg into it with care to keep it whole.

Have ready boiled spinach and mix a little cream sauce or a cheese sauce with it. Put it on the egg, leaving the yellow exposed. A few dabs of butter about and crumbled cracker crumbs, and if you wish, grated cheese at your discretion. Bake it in a moderate oven till the white but not the yellow hardens. It deserves to be rated with other Florentine works of art.

SCRAMBLED EGGS AND ASPARAGUS

20 small green asparagus
7 or 8 eggs
Butter
Salt, pepper, parsley
Tablespoon of cream

Cut the asparagus in small pieces,— about as big as peas. Your stew pan, with half a cup of water in it, and a little butter, salt, and pepper, receives the pieces of asparagus and they cook 25 minutes.

Have the eggs beaten, and put in proper salt and pepper, a little chopped parsley, and a bit of butter, and the cream. Mix the asparagus with these, and scramble them.

CALAS 'TOU' CHAUD'

1 cup of sugar
2 eggs
1 cup of boiled rice
2 cups of flour
2 teaspoons of baking powder
Lard

Mix the yolks of the eggs with the sugar, rice, flour, and baking powder. When they are thoroughly assembled, add the whites of the eggs well beaten, and give it all a final stirring.

Have some deep grease at hand, sizzling in your frying-pan, and drop the mixture from a spoon into the grease. They emerge golden brown, light, and luscious. Drain them on butcher's paper, sprinkle them with powdered sugar.

JAMBALAYA

1 tablespoon of lard
1 teaspoon of flour
2 tomatoes, large (or ½ a can)
1 cup of rice
1 onion, ½-green pepper, bit of garlic, salt, pepper, red pepper
Shrimp, or ham, or oysters,—or almost anything!

An iron pot is essential, one that can be well covered. Brown the chopped onion in the lard, then stir in the flour. Next, the chopped up tomatoes, the chopped shrimp, or ham, or what-not, and let them cook while you stir carefully. Now the boiling water, and give the things ten minutes or so to simmer.
Have the rice well washed, and put it in; let it boil without stirring long enough to be thoroughly done. Keep it covered well during these cooking processes.

JAMBALAYA LAFITTE

1 tablespoon of flour
1 tablespoon of lard
1 slice of ham (diced cold chicken, if available)
1 lb. of chaurice
2 tablespoons of tomatoes
1 lb. of raw shrimp (peeled)
1 handful of chopped onions
Garlic to taste, red pepper pod
1 cup of raw rice
1½ cups of water
1½ doz. oysters
Chopped green onion tops and parsley, salt, pepper

Be sure to use the old iron pot, with the cover to it.
First the roux of lard and flour, which must brown lightly. Then add the ham,—and the chicken, if you happen to have some. Then the tomatoes, shrimp and chaurice. (That last is an old French Market specialty; but it may be had elsewhere; it is a very highly seasoned sausage.)
This must be covered and let cook 20 minutes.
Then in go the onions, pepper, garlic, rice, and water, and cooking must go on, under cover always, till the rice is well done. Then add the oysters, and when their edges curl, this marvel of dishes is finished.
Dorothy Dix, eating at Lafitte's old rendezvous, now the bayou home of Mrs. Helen Schertz, said, "One should go on one's knees to eat this."
One of its numerous virtues is that it is just as good the next day.

PAIN PERDU (LOST BREAD)

2 cups of milk
¼ of a cup of sugar
2 eggs
Bread
Bread crumbs
Lemon peel or orange-flower water

Slice the bread, cut the crust off and cut the slices round or in strips.
Put the sugar in the milk, add a little scraped lemon peel or orange flower water, and a pinch of salt. Let the milk boil a few minutes.
Dip the pieces of bread in the milk, squeeze them gently to keep them from being too moist, and dip them into the eggs, which must be waiting well-beaten, then dip them in buttered bread crumbs.
Drop them next into piping hot grease, fry them, and sprinkle them with sugar.
The French serve them as a dessert, but they are very nice to give a sweet touch with meats that like such accompaniments.

PAIN PERDU CREOLE

1 egg
Nutmeg
Milk—about 1 cup
Sugar—2 good tablespoons
Bread

Beat the egg and sugar together. Add the nutmeg and milk. If the bread is not quite soft and fresh, use a little more milk.
Dip the bread in, squeeze it out a little, and fry it in deep hot fat.

EGGS EN MATELOTE

3 glasses of red wine (cooking wine)
3 glasses of water
Eggs
1 onion, thyme, bay leaf, garlic, parsley, salt, pepper
2 tablespoons of butter
2 tablespoons of flour

All the herbs, onions, garlic, chopped up, of course. They join the water and wine in a saucepan and cook 15 minutes. Then fish out the herbs, onion, et cet., and let the eggs poach in the sauce.
Take the eggs out and put them where they will remain hot, and let your sauce cook down a little. Then stir in the butter and the flour, let it cook a little, and then pour it over the eggs. They should appear surrounded by croutons fried in butter.

CHEESE SOUFFLE

6 eggs
¼ lb. American cheese
1 cup of milk
½ tablespoon of butter
Pepper, salt

Grate the cheese. Beat the eggs, yolks and white separately, vigorously. Add the cheese, the butter, and milk, and pour into a buttered pan. It is ready for ½ an hour in a moderate oven, and is a nice bit for luncheon.

BAKED HOMINY

"ain' no dish tasty twice runnin': gotta put a new face on ter be pleasin'."

Your cold grits (small hominy) with an egg or two (depending on the amount of grits) stirred into it, a little milk to bring it to a soft consistency, a little salt, and some butter, put in a baking pan and browned in the oven is a most palatable dish,—especially with grillades.

"some sez de good Lawd mek Friday fer a penance. Huh! Ef da's so, howcome he mek so many good fishes and let folks know so many tasty ways ter dish 'em up?"

BOILED FISH

The ritual of boiled fish is simple, but sacred. Its essentials are many herbs.

Red fish, red snapper, sheepshead, trout
Onion, pinch of thyme, bay leaf, cloves, allspice, cayenne, salt, pepper

The fish is well washed. It must not be too small. 2 lbs. is a good minimum. It is massaged well with salt and a little lemon. The herbs and seasonings in liberal quantities are put in enough water to cover the fish amply. Let the water boil a few minutes with all its seasonings before putting in the fish.

According to some culinary dictators, the fish should be wrapped about with a cord only before being put in the water. Others advocate wrapping it about with an old napkin or a muslin cloth.

In either case, place a little muslin bag full of herbs inside the fish, it heightens the flavor.

Old Creole tradition insists that the fish be slashed across in two or three places, on each side, to prevent its puffing up and to allow the seasoning to permeate it well.

The finished product is delicious with drawn butter sauce, caper sauce, egg sauce, and various others.

COLD RED FISH BARATARIA

4-lb. red snapper (or red fish)
Onions, garlic, pinch of thyme, bay leaves, parsley, salt, pepper, cayenne
6 tomatoes
4 green peppers
1 can of asparagus tips
Pimentoes, mayonnaise, celery

Boil as advised above, and put on ice to harden.

Put it on your best platter and treat it like a cake: ice it solidly with mayonnaise and surround it with quartered tomatoes, sprinkled with chopped celery, alternating with clusters of asparagus tips ringed with green peppers. Arrange strips of pimento across the mayonnaise, according to your best artistic instincts; sprinkle chopped parsley over everything. It looks too beautiful to eat, but too good to resist. With a few potato chips, it is Sunday night supper complete.

TROUT LOUISIANE

2 or 3 lbs. of trout (or red-fish, or red snapper)
2-inch slice of bread
½ cup of milk
3 tablespoons of butter
2 eggs
Salt, pepper, cayenne, pinch of thyme, onion
Sauce:
  1 cup of flour
  ½ cup of butter
  1½ cups of milk
  1 can of mushrooms
  Pepper, salt, sherry flavoring

Boil the fish according to the rites prescribed above. Chill it, skin it, and break it up well.

Take the inside of the bread (discarding the crust), soak it, press it dry, and put it with the fish. Next come the milk, the salt, and pepper, and cayenne.

Next, melt the butter, beat the eggs, and add these to the collection. Pour it into molds, put the molds into a pan of water, the pan into a hot oven for a good fifteen minutes baking.

Now for the sauce: melt the butter. Add salt and pepper to the flour and stir it slowly into the butter. Then the milk, still stirring. Let it boil 2 minutes, then add mushrooms and some sherry flavoring.

RED FISH CREOLE

3-lb. (or more) red fish, red snapper, or sheepshead
5 tablespoonfuls of olive oil
8 tomatoes (1 large can)
Garlic, onion, parsley, lemon, salt, pepper, cayenne

Massage the fish thoroughly with olive oil, salt and pepper. Gash it across each side in 2 or 3 places. Put it in a baking pan and pour over it a generous tablespoon of olive oil. Cook it in a moderate oven until tender.

Meanwhile, take your frying pan and put into it 4 tablespoons of olive oil, with chopped up tomatoes and herbs, and liberal seasoning. Fry this for 5 minutes. Add it to the baked fish and hurry the dinner-hour, for a treat is awaiting you.

RED FISH FARCI

3-lb. (or more) red fish, red snapper, or sheepshead
Flour
1 teaspoonful of olive oil
1 cup of toasted bread crumbs
2 eggs (the yolks)
1 tablespoon of butter
1 tablespoon of lard
6 tomatoes
3 cups of boiling water
2 onions, green onion top, clove of garlic, bay leaf, ½ green pepper, salt, pepper, cayenne

Slash the fish 2 or 3 times across each side. Rub it well with salt, then with flour.

Wet the bread crumbs, then squeeze them dry. Cup up the herbs, green pepper, garlic, mix them with the bread crumbs, add salt and pepper at will. Fry this for a few minutes in the butter and lard, and you have a stuffing for your fish. Put it in the fish and sew it up.

Out with your baking pan. Put enough boiling water to cover the bottom and set the fish in it, and the pan in the oven.

Chop up an onion, garlic, green onion top, with tomatoes, and seasoning, and after the fish has a good start towards baking, put them in with it. Also, any excess stuffing.

A 3-lb. red snapper should bake about an hour, and be basted often. The larger the fish, the longer the baking.

RED SNAPPER DE LUXE

3-lb. red snapper
1 tablespoon of butter
1 tablespoon of flour
1 cup of cream
2 eggs (yolks)
Onion, lemon, green pepper, bay leaf, pinch of thyme, cayenne, salt, pepper

The first step is boiling, as prescribed above. Chill the fish on ice. Step No. 2 begins: Skin the fish and break it into bits. Do some chopping,—the onion, green pepper, parsley. Work the flour and butter together, and put the cream with it, add the chopped onion, pepper, herbs, and seasoning, and the yolks of the eggs.

Add all this to the chopped fish, mix it together nicely, and put it in a butter-ed mold. Cover it with waxed paper. Put the baking pan in a pan of water and stow it away in a moderate oven for 45 minutes. It demands a Hollandaise sauce. And it assures your reputation as a hostess.

CREOLE TROUT MARGUERY

"moughty-lak sometimes kin be good es de-same."

2 lbs. of red snapper
3 hard-boiled eggs
2 lbs. of boiled shrimp
½-lb. of American cheese
1 can of mushrooms
1 tablespoon of chopped truffles.
2 tablespoons of butter
1½ tablespoons of flour
1 cup of cream
Onion, parsley, bay leaf, green pepper, salt, pepper, cayenne

The red snapper (or his ilk) starts with boiling, as previously described. It is cooled on ice, then skinned, and broken in pieces.

Grate the cheese; chop up the eggs and the shrimp, and put them all together in a baking pan.

Add salt and pepper to the flour. Have the butter bubbling in a saucepan, and add it to the flour with seasoning, stirring diligently. Next the cream with more stirring. Let it boil 2 minutes.

Pour this in your waiting baking pan, with the mushrooms and truffles and let it cook in a moderate oven for about an hour. The Boulevard des Bons Enfants could not offer you better.

Small clams or oysters are a great addition, mixed with the shrimp.

ESCALLOPED TROUT

2 lbs. of tenderloin trout (or red fish, or snapper)
6 strips of bacon
1 doz. oysters
½ cup of toasted bread crumbs
2 tablespoons of butter
1 tablespoon of olive oil
½ green pepper, parsley, salt, pepper, cayenne

Shred the chilled boiled fish, not too small. Lay it in a baking dish, pour the olive oil over it, and put little dabs of butter on it.

Put a layer of oysters, then of the green peppers, salt, pepper, a dash of cayenne. Bread crumbs and bacon for a top layer, and each layer must have dabs of butter.

Twenty-five minutes in a good oven will turn this out a finished product and a rich one!

COLD SPANISH FISH

3 lbs. of tenderloin trout in slices (or red snapper, or red fish)
3 tablespoons of olive oil
2 tomatoes (or ½ small can)
1 green pepper
1 tablespoon of flour
1 egg
2 onions, cloves of garlic, pinch of thyme, ginger, celery, green onion top, salt, pepper

The celery, onions, garlic, and herbs must all go under the knife. Out with the frying pan and into it with the olive oil and the chopped up ingredients just mentioned, to cook slowly a few minutes.

Now the fish, slice by slice, side by side. Cover it over with water and season it well with salt, pepper, ginger, and a dash of cayenne. Cut up the tomatoes and peppers, add them to the fish, and let them boil smartly for ½ an hour. Meanwhile, busy yourself with the yolk of an egg and the flour, beating them together, with just enough water to make them smooth.

When the fish is done, take it out and set it aside on the serving-dish. Pour the egg sauce into the frying pan and let it cook mildly there a few minutes. Strain it and pour it over the fish.

Let it all cool and serve it at your leisure.

COURTBOUILLON

"ef de Lawd wuz mekkin' Heb'n jes fo' de mouf, de ribber Jo'dan 'ld be runnin' Cou'bi'yon."

8 slices of red fish (or red snapper)
1 pint of olive oil
4 onions, 3 cloves of garlic
6 tomatoes
5 sweet peppers
1 quart of white wine (cooking wine)
Black pepper, salt, cayenne, cloves, a pinch of thyme

Put herbs, cloves, nutmeg, a dash of cayenne, in the olive oil. Rub the fish with salt and some black pepper, and let it stand in the seasoned olive oil for ½ hour or so. Now to business. Pour off the olive oil into a large saucepan. Crush utterly the onions and garlic, put them in the oil and leave them to brown.

Devote yourself to chopping the tomatoes and peppers.

Put them, with the wine, into the saucepan, and give them five minutes together there.

Dredge the fish in dry flour and lay the slices side by side in the boiling sauce. 15 minutes of simmering there, and you have a culinary masterpiece before you.

COURTBOUILLON CHEF MENTEUR

3 lbs. of sliced red fish (or red snapper)
1 tablespoon of lard
2 tablespoons of flour
6 tomatoes (1 large can)
3 quarts of water
Onion, garlic, clove, thyme, bay leaf, salt, pepper, red pepper pod, 1 lemon

Prepare to chop,—tomatoes, onions, garlic, all your herbs.

Make a roux, stirring the flour smoothly into the hot lard. Put in your chopped herbs, garlic, and onions. Give them a few minutes together, then add the tomatoes, then the water. Season judiciously and let it boil 5 minutes.

Put in the fish, the slices side by side like domitory beds. Add the juice of a lemon, and give it 10 minutes.

Serve in all the glory of its sauce, on toast, with sliced lemon set about the dish.

This dish should be called Cleopatra: it has so many variations. Wine flavoring is a help, of course. Sweet peppers are an addition highly recommended. Some artists of the frying pan recommend pouring hot vinegar over the slices of fish.

FISH ST. MARTIN

3-lb. red fish (or snapper)
1 or 2 lbs. boiled shrimp
2 doz. oysters
1 good cup of bread crumbs
1 can of mushrooms
2 tablespoons of butter
Salt, pepper, onion juice, parsley, ½ green pepper, onion

Pour the liquor of the oysters in a large baking pan. Rub the fish well with salt, and pepper and put it in, with the seasoning, and the chopped onion and pepper.

Peel the shrimp and add them to the collection.

Put it in the oven and let it bake about 15 minutes.

Take it out and add a cupful of fine bread crumbs, some mushrooms, and dot lumps of butter around.

Just a few minutes before serving add the oysters: they cannot stand long cooking. This dish is worthy a saint's name: it is so good!

BOUILLABAISSE LOUISIANE

"some things talks ha'd, but does easy."

3 lbs. of red fish, 3 lbs. of red snapper
6 fresh tomatoes (or 1 can)
½ pint of olive oil
2 onions, 3 cloves of garlic, parsley, thyme, bay leaf
½ lemon
cayenne
Pinch of Spanish saffron, salt, pepper, 1 pint of water

Pulverize the herbs together with the garlic: this is to be a dish full of taste.

Slash across the sides of the fish, rub it well with salt and pepper, and with herbs, and let it stand for a while in a covered dish.

Chop up the onions and put them in a mammoth saucepan with hot olive oil. Lay the slices of fish in side by side, cover them up, and let them cook gently about 10 minutes. But do not wholly desert them: turn them from time to time.

Now out with the fish, and give the tomatoes a turn. Slice them, and put them in, then the sliced lemon, the water, and seasoning.

Let it boil well, then put back the fish, side by side, and let them cook five minutes.

Take out a little of the sauce and mix it with a pinch of Spanish saffron. Just before the grand finish, add it to the fish, and serve your bouillabaisse on toast,—to the delight and admiration of all.

BOUILLABAISSE DE BAYOU

"plen'y diff'ent roads takes yo' into town; de same fer cookin',—mighty few things got a jes'-one-way."

4 lbs. of red fish (9 slices)
½ pint of olive oil
4 sweet peppers
2 tablespoons of flour
1 pint of fish stock
1 pint of white wine (cooking wine)
Salt, pepper onion, pinch of thyme, parsley

Crush up the herbs. Give the fish a massage, first with salt and pepper, then well with the herbs.

Put the oil in a frying pan and add the pepper, onion, herbs, et cet. well chopped, with the flour and the white wine and fish stock.

Let it boil 10 minutes, and add a pinch of Spanish saffron. Put in the fish, cover it, and let it cook slowly for 20 minutes.

Fish stock: Fish stock can be made by boiling the fish head in water seasoned with herbs and sliced onions. Boil until the water is reduced by at least a quarter of its original quantity.

TROUT MELANIE

1 3-lb. trout
1½ doz. oysters
1½ doz. shrimp
1 can of mushrooms
1 cup of flour
1 cup of butter
1 cup of white wine
3 eggs
1 large onion, thyme, bay leaf, parsley, salt, pepper

Rub the fish well with salt and pepper, lay it in a pan, and cover it with sliced onion and mushrooms, and let it stand an hour.

Make a roux adding flour slowly to melted butter, and stirring always. Add the oyster water and the liquid drained from the fish, and let it boil. Put in chopped parsley liberally, herbs, and seasoning.

Now the wine. Let it come just to a boil again; remove and stir in the 3 whole eggs. Take the onions off the fish, and halve the mushrooms.

Now, at last, the baking dish, a presentable one as the fish must appear at the table in it. Lay the fish in it, cover it with bread crumbs then, in succession, a layer of mushrooms, with, if you like a little chopped ripe olives, then a layer of oysters, and of shrimp.

The gravy over all, and bake.

"ez meny ways yo' min' kin turn, dat's how meny ways yo' kin mek a dish wid oysters."

The versatility of oysters is truly as elastic as the ingenuity of the cook.

BROILED OYSTERS: There is little mystery to the broiling process. The oysters should be drained, dried, sprinkled with a little salt and red pepper, and dipped in melted butter. Then, broiled in butter in the broiler; served with chopped parsley and bits of lemon, on toast or with congenial adjuncts, they are too good to be thought of unless soon to be enjoyed!

EN BROCHETTE: Long skewers, silver or aluminum, rare in the average cuisine, are necessary. The oysters are prepared as for broiling, but are run on skewers, the oysters alternating with strips of bacon cut oyster length. Minced parsley and lemon and drawn butter are an essential final touch. The same charm of flavor without the complication of skewers is found in

OYSTERS WRAPPED: The broiling preparation again,—drying, salt, pepper, cayenne. Then each voluptuous oyster is encased in a strip of bacon, held in place by a bit of toothpick. This is broiled, and served on toast with drawn butter and minced parsley over it, and bits of lemon about. Toothsome and so rich!

ON THE SHELLS: A favorite way of serving. Preliminary to the broiling process, the oysters may be sauté a minute or two in a saucepan with a tablespoon of butter, with chopped green onion top, minced parsley and herbs. Then they are put back in their shells, (which must, of course, be well cleaned) sprinkled with toasted bread crumbs, dabbed with butter, and then broiled. Slices of lemon are an essential touch to serving.

BAKED OYSTERS: Connoisseurs roll their eyes in the delight of this very simple dish. The oysters are left in their shells, well-cleaned, and put in a hot oven for 20 minutes. They open,—perhaps in astonishment at the unaccustomed heat. The shallow shells are removed and the oysters are left in the deeper ones, which are put on hot plates and served with despatch. Minced parsley may be sprinkled over them.

Each guest may be allowed to season his own, with butter, salt, pepper, and lemon juice. Or the attentive host may provide a sauce of drawn butter, with chopped parsley, lemon juice, salt, pepper, and a bit of cayenne.

FRIED OYSTERS: The delight of the result is not to be measured by the simplicity of the process! The oysters are drained, sprinkled with salt, pepper, and a bit of cayenne, rolled in bread crumbs (or meal if preferred) and dropped into deep sizzling lard When they brown beautifully golden, they should be put on brown 'butcher's' paper to absorb the

grease. They demand sliced lemon, quartered pickles, and parsley for garnishing. There is a cult that solemnly demands a complication of this process, as follows: one egg is beaten up in a ½ pint of milk, and the oysters are dipped in this prior to the bread crumb stage, acquiring perhaps a bit more delicacy of flavor to the sensitive palate.

OYSTERS ST. PIERRE

3 doz. oysters
1 tablespoon of flour
1 tablespoon of butter
1 cup of milk
2 eggs (yolks)
½ onion, bit of chopped onion top, parsley, salt, pepper, cayenne

Boil the oysters in their juice till they grow puffy. Then take them out and chop them up.

Work the flour and butter together. Put the milk in a double boiler and as it comes to a boil, stir in the flour and butter, with restraint.

Next come the yolks of the eggs, well beaten; then the seasoning, parsley, herbs; also chopped mushrooms, if your generosity goes so far; green peppers as well delight many tastes. Then the oysters.

This is all stirred up together ready for baking. Deep shells are effective for this, but the taste is just as delicious in ramekins, or even in a usual baking dish. Cracker or bread crumbs are sprinkled over the top, dabs of butter administered. 5 minutes baking brings out a delicious finished product.

SPANISH OYSTERS

3 doz. oysters
1 tablespoon of butter
2 tablespoons of flour
1 can of tomatoes
Onion, parsley, green onion top, pickle, sweet pepper, celery, salt, pepper, cayenne, Worcestershire sauce

Fry the chopped onion in the butter, and beware of the treacherous tendency to burn!

Add the flour and let it brown; then season, and add the chopped herbs, onion, grated celery, and sliced pickle. Mushrooms, if you will. Then the oysters. A touch of Worcestershire at the last minute is a happy one.

OYSTERS ROCKERFELLER

"dey tells me dis-hyah Mistah Roccke-fellah pow'ful rich; dat so, dey right to name dis dish arter him, 'cause who eat it feel as good as ef he was rich."

2 doz. oysters
Bacon
Bread crumbs
Spinach
½ lb. of butter
Parsley, green onion top, lemon, salt, pepper, cayenne

Wash fresh oysters and clean them thoroughly. Put each oyster on its shell. Chop up the shallot tops, and parsley, and mix them well with the butter, adding salt, pepper, and cayenne.

Put some of this mixture on top of each oyster. Then bits of minced bacon, then a little cooked spinach. Over this, sprinkle sparingly bread crumbs, browned and buttered.

Run the oysters in a hot oven and let them stay till they begin to swell a little, —about five minutes.

In New Orleans restaurants, the shells are set in a shallow pan which has ice cream salt in it, to preserve the heat; and the oysters are served in it, about ¾ dozen to each pan. Very crusty bread is recommended to go with it.

OYSTERS GRANDE DAME

4 doz. medium oysters
4 tablespoons of olive oil
2 tablespoons of butter
1 lemon
Parsley, shallots, 1 clove of garlic, salt, pepper, tabasco
1 wine-glass of white wine (cooking wine)

Put 2 tablespoons of the olive oil in a flat baking dish, and arrange the oysters in it neatly.

Pour 2 more tablespoons of oil over them. Chop the herbs, shallots, parsley, garlic, very well. There should be at least 4 tablespoons of ground shallots and as much parsley. Sift flour over it all, and put half a dozen goodly lumps of butter about the top. Squeeze the juice of a lemon over it, then the Worcestershire, salt, pepper, and about a half of the oyster liquor. Add the white wine.

Bake in a hot oven about 15 or 20 minutes. Then run the dish under the flame to brown.

Good crusty French bread should accompany this dish,—not crackers, nor white bread.

ESCALLOPED OYSTERS

2 doz. oysters
1 cup of oyster liquor
¾ cup of milk
1 cup of cracker crumbs
1 cup of bread crumbs
4 tablespoons of butter
Salt, pepper, cayenne

This is a Yankee method, I have heard; but it has its followers here.

The butter is melted and mixed with the bread and cracker crumbs. A layer of this is placed in the bottom of the baking dish; then a layer of oysters, sprinkled with salt, pepper, and cayenne. Then a layer of crumbs, with little dots of butter here and there; another layer of oysters, with seasoning, and the final layer of crumbs, with, on each layer, scatterred dabs of butter.

CRAB MEAT RAMEKINS

"crab aint' nuthin' to de eye; but in de mouf ain't nuthin' pass him."

1 lb. of crab meat
2 tablespoons of butter
⅓ pint of cream
1 can mushrooms
3 sour pickles (or 1 tablespoon of capers)
3 hard-boiled eggs
Chopped parsley, sweet pepper, salt, white pepper, dash of cayenne
Sherry flavoring

Ply your knife into the mushrooms, peppers, eggs, parsley, pickles, (capers) and chop them all up. Put them all together with the crab meat.

Melt the butter and pour it in; then the milk. Season it well. A little paprika with the other seasoning suits many tastes.

Let it all reach the boiling point, then take it off the fire and add sherry flavoring.

It must then go into shells or ramekins, sprinkled with bread crumbs with bits of butter, and installed in the oven for 15 minutes. It can even serve as a piece de resistance for an informal luncheon, if it is baked in a baking dish. It is good even without the sherry flavoring,—but so much better with!

CRAB MEAT A L'ESPAGNOL

1 lb. of crab meat
1 tablespoon of butter
1 cup of flour
3 tablespoons of olive oil
2 onions, 3 cloves of garlic,
3 tomatoes (or 1 small can)
Parsley, celery, green onion top, green pepper, salt, pepper
3 cups of water, and sherry flavoring, or 1 cup of water and 1 cup red wine

Begin with the olive oil, onion, and garlic,—of course, since the idea is Spanish! Cut the onions and garlic fine, and put them with the olive oil to brown (the final product is as good as it smells!)

Chop again,—all the herbs and seasonings, and tomatoes, and add them with the flour and water to the browned onions and garlic and butter; salt, pepper, cayenne.

Let it all boil 30 minutes, then strain it, add the sherry flavoring. Put in the crab meat and let it cook ten minutes. Serve on crisp buttered toast and be thankful to Valencia, whence this is said to have come.

STUFFED CRABS

1 lb. of crab meat
8 shells
Bread
1 egg
1 tablespoon of butter
Parsley, bit of thyme, green onion top, green pepper, cayenne, salt, pepper

Boil the crabs in seasoned water, well salted.

Soak the bread,—about ½ the quantity of the crab meat—in water and squeeze it dry.

Chop the onion and brown it in the butter; then brown the bread with it. Mix the crab meat and seasoning with the bread and onions on the fire,—just mix it, then remove it.

Break the egg into the mixture, add a little butter, and a bit of cayenne. Put the mixture into the shells, sprinkle over with bread crumbs, with a dab of butter on each, and let it stay in the oven about five minutes.

A little hard-boiled egg is good, mixed with the dressing, if you wish. Creamed potatoes may be used instead of part of the bread crumbs, too.

CREAMED CRAB MEAT

1 lb. of meat of boiled crabs
2 tablespoons of butter
2 tablespoons of flour
3 hard-boiled eggs (yolks)
1 cup of cream
Salt, pepper, green onion top, parsley, paprika, lemon, cayenne.

Mash the yolks of the eggs with salt, pepper, paprika, cayenne, lemon.

Make a roux, stirring the flour smoothly into the melted butter. Add the cream, the mashed yolks, seasoning, chopped parsley, and let it cook till it thickens a little. Then add the crab meat and let it cook a few minutes longer. Take it off and add sherry flavoring.

Favorite additions to this happy framework are chopped sweet peppers, and a little chopped pimento. Minced parsley over it sparingly is good. It is a reliable chafing dish resource. It may be served in pattie shells (without the tops). And it is delicious in English biscuits, the thick ones,—the centers hollowed out and filled with this.

BOILED SHRIMP

"swimpses' tas'e is lak some fok's conscience: somebody else got to put it into 'em."

Mandy, as usual, is right: an egg without salt is as savory as shrimp boiled without proper and ample seasoning.

The water must be strongly salted; then liberally add to it pepper, cayenne, a pepper pod; cloves; bay leaf; a little thyme; celery, celery tops,—whatever gives a 'taste.' Let all these boil well for a bit; then put in the shrimp, and let them boil for 20 minutes.

SHRIMP BALLS

1 lb. of shrimp
1 cup of bread crumbs
1 teaspoon of butter
1 tablespoon of lard
2 tablespoons of flour
2 to 3 cups of water
Shallot tops, green pepper, parsley, salt, pepper, cayenne

Boil the shrimp, peel them, and chop them up well. Season them with the chopped onion top, parsley, green pepper, et cet.

Melt a teaspoon of butter and add to

your bread crumbs,—which are, of course, rolled and toasted.

Add these to the shrimp combination. Shape it into cones or balls, and fry them in deep fat.

Take them out and add flour in the saucepan, let it brown, then add water. A little slow cooking will thicken it up, and then the croquettes go back in, and everything cooks together slowly, for another quarter of an hour. A little boiled rice in with the shrimp is a pleasant variation.

SHRIMP LOUISIANE

1 lb. of shrimp
1 tablespoon of butter
1 tablespoon of flour
4 tomatoes (or 1 small can)
1 cup of water
1 onion, green pepper, parsley, shallot tops, pepper, salt, cayenne
½ tablespoon of Worcestershire

Chop the onion fine and let it simmer in the butter. Stir the flour smoothly and let it brown.

Chop up the tomatoes, parsley, herbs, and the rest, and add them one and all to the browned flour and onions. Season generously.

Add the shrimp (boiled and peeled) and let them cook for 20 minutes on a mild fire.

Take them off and put in Worcestershire. Your respect for shrimp will shoot to zenith.

Note: Crabs, shrimp, and oysters, may be used interchangeably in many of these recipes.

"good vittles on de table meks good comp'ny 'round erbout it."

GRILLADES LOUISIANE

2 veal rounds
1 tablespoon of lard
2 tablespoons of flour
2 cups of water
2 tablespoons of tomato paste
1 onion, 2 green peppers, bay leaf,
   thyme, salt, pepper, cayenne

Select good veal rounds, not too thin. Fry them; take them out and cut them in pieces suitable for individual service; salt, pepper, cayenne.

Now a roux,—Stir in the flour smoothly to the hot lard. When it browns add the water.

This is the time for the onion, peppers, bay leaf, and thyme, well cut up together; add them with the tomato paste and parsley, and liberal seasoning. When this browns, back with the veal, and let it all simmer half an hour.

The tomato paste is not vital, but most advisable.

Serve with rice, or with baked hominy, or Pain Perdu, and, voila, madame, a dish to delight any Creole or any human with a discerning palate. And not dear, either.

GRILLADES JARDINIERES

2 veal rounds
2 tablespoons of butter
Boiled potatoes, carrots, beets, green
   peas, parsley,
1 teaspoon tomato catsup (or tablespoon of tomato paste)

Prepare the grillades as above; then cut them in smaller pieces.

Chop the potatoes, carrots, and beets, and put them in a covered baking dish with the chopped grillades and some of the gravy, and tomato catsup. Little dabs of butter on top. Set the baking dish in a pan of water in the oven, and give it 15 minutes.

A few mushrooms and a little wine flavoring add elegance and flavor; but at its simplest it is worth while.

FLANK STEAK DE LUXE

'co'n fiel' pass fo' quality ef she got plenty fixin's,—en a po' piece o' meat is good ez de bes' ef it got de right some'p'n wid it."

Flank steak
1 tablespoon of flour
2 tablespoons of butter
3 tablespoons of vinegar
1 teaspoon of mustard, onion, paprika,
   thyme, salt, pepper, cayenne
2 cups of water

Cut the steak in pieces for individual service.

Chop up the onion, brown it in the butter, and take it out. Dredge the pieces of steak in flour and fry them in this same butter, and put them aside.

Now for the gravy. Put in the saucepan the flour, vinegar, mustard, salt, pepper, and paprika; then the water. Put back the meat, and, if you have that virile taste, the onion, too.

Cover up the frying pan and let its contents simmer about ½ hour, or until the meat is tender.

No fine cut of meat could taste better.

GRILLADES PIQUANTES

1 round steak
1 tablespoon of lard
2 tablespoons of flour
3 tomatoes
2 teaspoons of vinegar
1 cup of water
Onion, clove of garlic, green pepper,
bay leaf, salt, pepper, cayenne

Season the grillades with salt, pepper, and cayenne, and cut them in pieces for individual service.

Slice the onion and brown it in the lard; take it out, and fry the meat there; then take the meat out.

Back with the onion, add flour smoothly, and let it brown. Then the peppers, garlic, bay leaf, all cut fine, and plenty of seasoning; then the sliced tomatoes.

When the tomatoes start cooking in earnest, put the grillades back in, and add the water and vinegar. Cover up the frying pan and let it have a quiet half hour of moderate cooking.

It has a little tang all its own.

Ground artichokes, please note, are always a happy addition to grillade gravies.

meat, poultry and game —❧{29}❧—

DAUBE ROAST

4 lbs. rump roast
Fat
Turnips, carrots, peas, a few leeks,
 shallots, 2 onions, clove of garlic,
 parsley, bay leaf, salt, pepper, cayenne

Beat the meat with the rolling pin to
make it tender. Make a number of slits
in it and rub into them salt, pepper, and
cayenne. It is good to put some of the
chopped herbs and onions in them and
(ah!) a bit of garlic.

Cut the fat in small pieces, and rub
seasoning into them, and put them into
the slits of the roast.

Your saucepan next,—a good old iron
one if possible. Melt some of the fat in
it,—eke it out with lard if necessary. Chop
the onions and brown them in this, then
put in the beef. Cover it up and let it
simmer After 10 minutes turn it over.

Your vegetables, the while, are neatly
cut. When the daube has browned a bit,
add them; also, boiling water, enough
to cover the daube. Let it have 3 hours
with a moderate fire, and you have a
mighty bulwark of a meal.

DAUBE A LA MODE

4 lbs. of rump roast
Fat
Vinegar, cooking wine, water
2 onions, 1 clove of garlic, bay leaves,
 thyme, parsley, salt, pepper, cayenne,
 ginger (Turnips, carrots, peas, a
 few leeks, shallots)

This starts out like the preceding. It
demands the addition, however, of a little
ginger with the herbs.

Again the old iron pot, and melt fat
in the bottom. Brown the sliced onions
in it, then put in the larded roast.

Now—pour around the roast the water,
cooking wine, and vinegar, in equal pro-
portions. A chopped lemon helps; also, a
piece of rye bread. You must start early
with this, for it takes its time. Let it
simmer three hours and baste it at intervals.

Diced vegetables, as indicated, added
early in the final process interchange
flavors with the roast and are delicious.

BRISKET

**"tek a little bit o' dis en' dat, en' yo' kin
put heart in a mighty flat piece o' meat,
come yo' knows how."**

The lowly brisket, known under the

aliases of soup-meat, or bouilli, is worth
notice. Mandy chooses one that has generous strips of fat, as the fat is rendered
in the soup. Any excess can be skimmed
off the soup; on the brisket, it becomes
jellied and adds to the flavor.

Served in slices, with a sauce Poydras,
or a sauce vinaigrette, it is excellent.
Cold boiled vegetables placed about it
give it dignity, and make it a substantial
supper dish,—a good one.

BRISKET MARINE

3 lbs. of soup brisket
1 tablespoon of lard
2 tablespoons of flour
4 tablespoons of olive oil
4 tablespoons of vinegar
1 lemon
Bay leaf, thyme, cloves, onion, garlic,
 salt, pepper, cayenne

Rub the brisket with salt, pepper, and a
bit of cayenne, with the garlic, and herbs.

Marinade it, that is, let it stand in the
ice box in a mixture of the oil, vinegar,
and lemon juice, with chopped onions
and herbs. It must spend several hours
in this savory bath.

Then let it simmer on the stove.
Make a roux, stirring the flour into the
lard, and add this to the soup meat, to
brown. Add boiling water, judiciously,
cover the saucepan, and let it simmer for
an hour, or an hour and a half. It will
find as much favor as a costly cut of meat.

STEAK ESPAGNOL

3 lbs. of tenderloin steak
Olive oil
1 onion, capers, parsley, sweet pepper,
 clove of garlic, salt, pepper, cayenne
2 cups of cooking wine

The steak must be baked in the oven—
a hot one—for ½ an hour. For this, it
is of course dredged in lard and sprinkled with pepper. When done—and it is
done when it is still rare—it is sliced
and ready for the really important touch,
the sauce.

The onions go in the saucepan with
enough olive oil to keep them from burning. Salt, pepper, cayenne, a little chopped green pepper, and the wine must be
added; then allow a good simmering,
enough well to concentrate the flavoring.

The parsley, capers, a piece of garlic,
must be well chopped, and with the salt,
are the final addition. Simple but rich.

ROAST BEEF BONHOMME

4 lbs. roast beef
1 tablespoon of lard
Some of the following:
   potatoes, peas, carrots, turnips, mustard greens, mushrooms, white onions
Bay leaf, thyme, parsley, salt, pepper

The round is rubbed with salt, pepper, and cayenne, and larded.

Brown the sliced onions in the lard, then put in the roast beef, add water and cover the saucepan. Let the beef cook until it is tender, but not too long: it should appear on the table a little rare.

A wise selection must be made of a congenial few of the vegetables mentioned. Have them cooked and drained, and piping hot. Season them, put a little butter over them, and set them about the roast.

This same combination is delicious served cold with a sauce vinaigrette, or a sauce Poydras.

STEAK WITH ONIONS

"dey's dis en dat 'bout a lot o' things but 'bout steak wid onions ain' mo'n one,— en' da's, it's good."

Beefsteak
1 pint of hot water
2 tablespoons of flour
1 tablespoon of butter
6 onions
Salt, pepper, cayenne

Broil the beefsteak separately. The onions finely sliced, go into a saucepan with the butter; add the water, and sift in a little flour. Let this stew until the onions are very tender. The broiled steak joins them, and they spend ten minutes together in the stew pan, and emerge a harmony for the palate.

Steak served with French fried potatoes, golden brown and crisp, is another joy for the gourmet.

CREOLE PORK CHOPS

Pork Chops
2 tablespoons of flour
1 tablespoon of lard
Green peppers, onions, bay leaf, parsley, green onion top, salt, pepper, red pepper pod

Roll the pork chops in flour, and fry them in a little lard, making a roux.

Pour in a cup of water, have the seasoning chopped up, add it, and let it all simmer slowly till the gravy is thick.

HASH

"dis worl's a place whah ev'ything's dependin' on somethin' else,—lak hash terday on yistiddy's dinner."

Nowhere is the hand of the virtuoso so much in evidence as in the composition of hash, wherein, truly, yesterday's dinner may undergo a glorious apotheosis or a sad degeneration, according to the skill of the artist. A suggestion:

Cold meat, chicken, beef, veal, what you will
1 tablespoon of butter
1 tablespoon of flour
Chopped potatoes (raw)
2 hard-boiled eggs
Sweet pepper, green onion top, onion, parsley, salt, pepper, cayenne
1 tablespoon of tomato paste

Meat, onion, onion top, potatoes, eggs, parsley, shallots, all undergo the chopping process, and are eventually mixed together. The meat may go in the grinder if you prefer.

The butter (or butter and lard, ½ of each) starts off in the stewpan, with a little flour stirred in smoothly. Then the chopped ingredients, to simmer a bit. Hot water is added judiciously, in proportion to the amount of meat as well as of guests to be served! Tomato paste, about 1 tablespoon, is advisable. Fifteen minutes longer on the stove will have harmonized all the ingredients and produced an excellent hash.

Not too many potatoes: about ½ as much as of meat.

Tomatoes, or carrots, or peas, or celery, and particularly ground artichokes, any one or more make acceptable additions.

DRY HASH

This starts out like the one above, but the amount of water is less. It must be put in the oven with dabs of butter on top and allowed to bake for about an hour.

VOL-AU-VENT

"a puhty name mought kin he'p a dish in de ear; but it got to do better'n dat fo' de mouf."

Vol-au-Vent is often only a pretty name that hash takes when it adopts the elegance of a pie-crust. Very good at that. The crust should be thin and crisp.

The hash may take furbelows worthy its new name: mushrooms particularly are a help. A strip or two of bacon goes palatably. There are many variations. The following is a very successful one:

Raw pork (or veal) 1 lb.
½ tablespoon of flour
1 tablespoon of lard
1 tablespoon of water
Shallot tops, parsley, sweet pepper, salt, pepper, red pepper pod, bay leaf
Grind the meat raw.

Make a roux of the flour and lard, add the water, and fry the meat 10 minutes. Add the seasoning and let it simmer a bit.

Have the baking dish lined with pastry, put in the meat, cover it with a layer of pastry, and let it bake until brown,—about 15 minutes.

MEAT CROQUETTES

Cold meat (roast veal, beef, or soup-meat)
2 tablespoons of milk
2 tablespoons of lard
1 tablespoon of flour
½ cup of stale bread
Green onion top, onion, sweet pepper, bay leaf, salt, pepper, cayenne, garlic

Much chopping,—first the meat, then the green onion top, sweet pepper, herbs, et cet. Mix them all together with the meat, and season liberally. Garlic is desirable.

Sculp the mixture into cones or balls, dip them in the milk, and sift flour over them lightly. Fry them in the deep grease, take them out and drain them. A good tomato sauce is excellent with them.

LIVER CROQUETTES

1 lb. of liver
1 tablespoon of flour
2 tablespoons of tomato paste
½ cup of water, ½ cup of cooking wine
2 onions, parsley, bay leaf, celery, salt, pepper, cayenne
Grind the liver very fine

Chop up all the liver, onions, parsley, herbs, and season well, and mix them together. Shape the mixture into balls or cones dipped in flour.

Mix the water, wine, and tomato paste and let the balls simmer in it for ½ an hour.

BAKED HAM, STYLE ROYAL

"makin' up a dinnah, it's lak ca'yin' a waitah in each han'; yo' gotta balance dis wid dat."

1 or more raw ham steaks
6 apples
6 sweet potatoes
½ box of seedless raisins
Sugar

Cajole from your butcher nice thick ham steaks.

Put them in a baking pan, the bottom of which is just covered with water. Peel and core 6 apples, stuff raisins in each. Peel and quarter nice yellow yams. Set these and the apples about the ham in the baking pan, and sprinkle granulated sugar, or brown sugar, liberally over it all. Cook in a slow oven.

This is a godsend for the harried hostess who has limited service. It is a piece de resistance so generous that only one side-dish need be served with it, so sweet that it obviates the advisability of a sweet dessert.

DAUBE GLACE, TECHE STYLE

2 lbs. of beef daube
1¼ lbs. of lean pork
½ lb. of boiled ham
Lard
2 large carrots
1 box of gelatine
Sliced onions, vinegar, cloves, bay leaf, cayenne, salt, pepper

Season the beef and pork with salt, pepper, and cayenne. Cover it with sliced onions, and vinegar, adding cloves, bay leaf and parsley. Let it stand an hour,— a 'marinade.'

Take it out, drain it, and fry it a golden brown. Dip out the onions from the 'marinade' liquor, and fry them brown.

Put the meat and onions, with the juice of the 'marinade' into a pot, fill it up with water, and let it boil 1 hour. Then add the ham and let it all boil till the meat seems ready to fall to pieces.

Now the carrots, sliced; then the gelatine, which has been properly soaked in cold water. Let it all come to a boil again, then remove it, and skim off the grease.

The end is near. Fish out the carrots, line a mold with them, and pour the contents of the pot into it; set it in the ice box for several hours. A final scraping of grease when it is put out on a plate, and it is ready to serve.

GREEN SHUTTER DAUBE GLACÉ

"ef yo' gonna stint yo' money, bes' not set yo' min' on a gol' chain: don' sta't out fo' a cold daube, lessen yo' gonna pay it time en' trouble."

After the first few experiences, it ceases to seem so formidable, and is truly a 'gol' chain' of dishes.

    3 lbs. of lean beef
    2 large knuckle bones (or 2 or 3 calf's
        feet)
    2 large onions, 2 carrots
    Caramel
    Celery tops, bay leaves, 10 cloves, small
        pod of garlic (garlic may be omitted)
    1 tablespoon (scant) of salt
    1 teaspoon of whole black pepper

Cover the bones with water and boil them for about 3 hours with the herbs, celery tops, et cet., tied in a bag; then add the meat and cook for 2 hours more.

Lift out the seasoning. Place the meat in a mold.

Strain the stock and color it with caramel; adding more salt and pepper if necessary. Pour it around the meat and when it is cold, place it on the ice for 24 hours.

All the grease will rise up on top of the mold. Scrape it off when you are ready to take out your daube. Invert it on the serving dish.

This recipe should be a classic: it is the gift of champion daube glacé makers, and it and the one above are the only two I have ever seen that do not meander through paragraphs calculated to quell the most ardent culinary enthusiasm.

HOT TAMALE PIE

    1 lb. ground beef
    1 can of tomatoes
    1 can of tomato paste
    1 cup of chopped onions
    ½ cup chopped celery, ½ cup chopped
        green peppers
    3 cups of cornmeal
    3 cups of water
    Salt, chili powder, red pepper, black
        pepper, butter

First, some little cornmeal cakes, thus: make a mush cooking the cornmeal with an equal quantity of water and salting it. When it is done, stir in a bit of butter, and let it cool a little. Then shape it into flat cakes. Now,—fry the chopped onions, celery, and pepper in hot lard. Add the meat and fry it.

When it is done, add the tomatoes, tomato paste, salt, peppers, and chili powder, and let it simmer together.

The baking dish, please. A layer of the meat mixture at the bottom, then a layer of the mush cakes; then meat again, alternately, until the dish is full. The top layer must be of meat. Bake it in a good oven. It is a stalwart dish, but delicious.

SWEETBREADS A LA REINE

    Sweetbreads
    1 tablespoon of butter
    1 tablespoon of flour
    ½ cup of cream
    1 cup of cracker crumbs
    1 egg
    Mushrooms
    Parsley, salt, pepper

Sweetbreads must, of course, be soaked in cold water for an hour, then cooked slowly 20 minutes in hot water with salt and vinegar in it; then drained and soaked in cold water again.

Make a cream sauce, stirring the flour into the butter, then adding the cream slowly, and seasoning. Let boil gently 2 minutes.

Take the cleaned parboiled sweetbreads, mix them with the mushrooms, and add them to the sauce. Mold them into cones, dip them into cracker crumbs, then egg, then again into cracker crumbs, and fry them in hot grease. It is like eating a savory cloud!

TRIPE

"yo' cain' tell de song by lookin' at de bird: ain' nobody'd recon a ol' ugly dish lak trip' 'ld go so sweet inter de mouf."

Tripe preliminaries are as essential as those of sweetbreads. Many waters must wash it; then it must be boiled for hours in water with a tablespoon of salt and a tablespoon of vinegar in it. Drained then, it is ready for service, in cooking.

TRIPE PIQUANTE

    2 lbs. of tripe
    1 tablespoon of butter
    1 tablespoon of flour
    1 teaspoon of vinegar (or lemon juice)
    Parsley, thyme, bay leaf, onion, garlic,
        carrot
    ½ cup of hot water

Chop up the herbs, garlic, carrot. Brown the chopped onion in the butter, then add herbs, and tripe.

Put in the tripe and vinegar, and after it has simmered a few minutes add the water. Season freely, and let it all simmer for twenty minutes.

"in de fiel' it's de fedders dat counts; on de table, it's de fixin'."

FRICASSEE OF CHICKEN PLAQUEMINE

3- or 4-lb. chicken
Flour,—or bread crumbs
¼ lb. of butter (or ½ butter, ½ lard)
Onion, green onion top, ½ green pepper, ground artichoke, salt, pepper, cayenne
1 cup of mushrooms
2 cups of hot water

Cut the chicken as for frying. Soaking an hour in warm water will whiten it. 1 tablespoon of vinegar in the water helps to make it tender. Massage the pieces with salt and pepper, and roll them in flour or bread crumbs.

Fry them in butter till they are brown, then take them out and set them aside.

The chopped onion, onion top, et cet. now go into the saucepan. Add the water and season freely. Let it all simmer a bit, then replace the chicken, add the mushrooms and let it all simmer for 45 minutes.

FRICASSEE OF CHICKEN POINTE COUPEE

3- or 4-lb. chicken
2 tablespoons of butter
2 tablespoons of flour
10 small onions
½ lb. of mushrooms (or 1 can)
1 egg (yolk)
2 glasses of warm water
Parsley, thyme, bay leaf, lemon, salt, pepper, cayenne

Age counts here as elsewhere: let your chicken be young. Cut as for frying and soak an hour in warm water with a little vinegar to whiten and make tender.

Put the butter in the saucepan, stir in the flour, and add the water, stirring faithfully. Add the chopped herbs and seasoning.

Now the pieces of chicken. Let it cook gently a bit, then put in the onions. A ½ of an hour before serving, add the mushrooms. Fresh mushrooms have to be blanched in boiling water, or they give a very swarthy complexion to the sauce.

When the chicken is cooked—at the end of an hour about—take it out and put it in the serving dish. Then put into your sauce a 'liaison' or binding, and the juice of ½ a lemon.

For the 'liaison', take 3 tablespoons of the gravy, and beat it up well with the yellow of the egg. Take the sauce off the fire, add the liaison, stir it well, and then add the juice of the ½ lemon. Pour the sauce over the chicken. Croutons fried in butter are very nice set about it.

Do not be discouraged by the length of the directions: there are more words than trouble, and the result is worth it all.

CHICKEN TIMBALES

"chicken ain' got mo'n one set o' fedders fo' de ba'n-ya'd; but dey plen'y diff'ent ways he kin come on de table."

1 cup of cooked chicken
⅔ cup of milk
2 tablespoons of bread crumbs
2 tablespoons of butter
2 eggs
Parsley, ½ onion, celery salt, salt, pepper, cayenne

Add the browned bread crumbs and milk to the melted butter in a saucepan and let them have 5 minutes there, with stirring.

Chop the chicken well, and of course the herbs, and add them. Then the eggs, yolks and whites beaten slightly.

Have buttered molds at hand in a pan of water, put the mixture in them and cover the molds with greased paper. Twenty minutes in the oven will turn them out for perfect service, with Bechamel sauce.

CHICKEN BALLS

"come-agen kin be better den new, wid a little doin."

Left over chicken
2 tablespoons of butter
½ tablespoon of flour
1 cup of scalded milk
Onion, shallot, thyme, parsley, celery, onion juice, green pepper, salt, pepper, cayenne

Cut up the onion, shallot, et cet., mix them with the chopped chicken and season well.

Stir the flour discreetly into the melted butter; add salt, pepper, and cayenne, and stir in the milk slowly. Let it boil calmly 2 minutes.

Add this to the chicken mixture, sculp it into balls, or cones, and fry them in deep grease.

LIVER RAMEKINS

1 cup of raw chicken liver
1 tablespoon of butter
½ tablespoon of cream
2 tablespoons of milk
3 eggs
Parsley, salt, pepper, cayenne, mushrooms at will

This is rich,—literally.
Press the liver through a colander. Beat up the yolks of the eggs, and add the cream and milk, melted butter, salt, pepper, and chopped parsley. Also mushrooms ad lib.
Put this mixture in buttered molds, covered with greased paper, put the mold in water, and let them bake 20 minutes.

CHICKEN A LA KING

"put somep'n good to somep'n good, en yo' boun' to git somep'n better ef yo' do it right."

2 cups of cooked chicken
2 tablespoons of butter
1½ tablespoons of flour
1 cup of cream
3 eggs
Green pepper, celery, pimento, mushrooms, carrot, green onion top, paprika, salt, pepper, cayenne
Sherry flavoring

Chop up the green pepper, celery et cet., and mix them with the chopped chicken meat. The pimento may be used or not, according to taste. Melt the butter in a saucepan, stir in the flour with care, and season. Now the cream, and let it all bubble quietly 2 minutes.
Add the chicken mixture and let it cook slowly about 15 minutes. Then the sherry flavoring.
Serve on toast, using sliced hard-boiled eggs as a garnish, and it is worthy its royal name.

FRIED CHICKEN MARINADE

1 chicken, frying size
4 tablespoons of olive oil
2 tablespoons of lemon juice
1 egg
½ cup of cracker crumbs
Salt, pepper, parsley, bay leaf, thyme, cayenne

Bake or boil the chicken and let it cool. Carve it, and cut it into strips. Put the strips in a bowl with olive oil, lemon juice, and seasoning, and set the bowl in the ice box, to stand over night, or at least several hours.
Dip the pieces of chicken in raw egg, then in cracker crumbs, and fry them in deep fat. Serve them with Sauce Piquante Parisienne.

CREAMED CHICKEN RAMEKINS

1 chicken
½ cup of cream
3 eggs (whites)
1 can of mushrooms
Celery salt, celery, green onion top, ½ green pepper, salt, pepper, cayenne
Pinch of soda

The meat is cut off the bones and minced finely. With this is mixed the chopped celery, et cet., and the mushrooms. (A little pimento is possible.)
Put the seasoning into the cream and add a pinch of soda to it.
Beat up the whites of the eggs, and mix everything together,—cream, minced meat, and eggs. Put the mixture into the ramikins, set them in a pan of water, and let them bake for 20 minutes. A happy start for any meal.

BROILED CHICKEN VENEZIA

"people is like chickens: whah dey's bes' ain' whah dey's happies'. A chicken he's a bothah on de do' step and a blessin' in de broilah."

Young chicken
Butter
Parmesan cheese
Salt, pepper, parsley

The usual procedure for broiling,—sprinkle the chicken with salt and pepper, dot with butter, and put in the dripping pan in the oven for 15 minutes. The fowl should be skin side down, of course, most of the time. When it is taken out for the last step, its turn in the broiler, sprinkle it liberally with Parmesan cheese. Serve it with a little drawn butter and chopped parsley sprinkled over it,—you will eat with gusto.

BROILED CHICKEN, with butter and chopped parsley, served with sauce Béarnaise is a piece of toothsome elegance, for which our restaurants are famous.

BAKED CHICKEN VENEZIA

1 boiled chicken
2 cups of white cream sauce
Asparagus tips
Mushrooms (½ a can)
Parmesan cheese
Celery salt, salt, pepper, parsley, cayenne

Cut up the chicken and put it with the asparagus tips, mushrooms, and the sauce, into a baking dish. Be liberal with the seasoning. A bit of chopped green pepper, and chopped green onion top may be included.

Sprinkle grated Parmesan cheese very thickly over the top. It will make a heart's desire of ramekins, if that suits your convenience better than the baking dish.

STUFFED CHICKEN

"a good roas'in' chicken he mek moughty good eatin', da's true; but wid a tasty sto' o' stuffiin' in him, he's dat good en twicet mo."

Large chicken
2 tablespoons of butter
2 cups of bread crumbs (or ½ bread, ½ cracker)
1 egg
Ground artichokes, onion, parsley, green onion top, green pepper, salt, pepper, cayenne
2 cups of water

Clean the hen well. It is better to have it killed the day before. Soak it an hour or so in warm water with a little vinegar for the sake of whitening and tenderness. Rub it with a little butter, salt, and pepper and flour. Soak the bread in water, squeeze it dry and mix it with the chopped up onion, and ground artichokes, and fry it all together in the butter, till it is dry. Then in with the chopped celery, parsley, onion, et cet., season it well; put in the egg well beaten, and 1 tablespoon of butter.

Stuff the chicken with this, and set it in the baking pan with 2 cups of water poured about it. Baste it often.

Extra dressing may cook in the pan with it and add to its excellence.

The above is the meagre outline of a dressing. No proper Creole cook could bear to have it without oysters; chopped pecans are an invaluable addition; so are clams. Chestnuts, if available, are good. the ground artichokes have something of their richness.

TURKEY excels with the same dressing, of course.

A substitute, rich and delicious, for cranberry sauce is this: pare and core several apples; in the center of each, put a little brown sugar and pieces of fried country sausage. Set the apples to bake in the same pan with the turkey.

CHICKEN WITH OLIVES

Have the chicken well cleaned and singed. Put it in the saucepan with a good piece of butter, and let it brown. Then take it out, and make a roux, by stirring in 2 tablespoons of flour slow and sure.

When this has browned in turn, add 2 cups of water, seasonings (thyme, chopped parsley, bay leaf); let these simmer a few minutes, then put back the chicken, and let it cook until done.

Have ready ½ lb. of olives. If they are peeled from the seeds spirally they will preserve their pristine oval forms. Arrange these around the chicken in the service platter and pour the sauce over it all.

CHICKEN MARENGO

Chicken (large frying size)
4 tablespoons of olive oil
½ lb. of mushrooms
Scant cup of cooking wine
2 shallots, parsley, salt, pepper

Prepare the chicken as for frying. Put the olive oil in a saucepan and let the pieces of chicken cook in it till they brown (about ¼ of an hour).

Have the mushrooms, the shallots (tops and all) and parsley chopped up together. Take a small saucepan, and put them in it with the cooking wine. Let it boil, then add 2 tablespoons of the oil in which the chicken was cooked.

Serve the chicken with the sauce poured over it, and with toast fried in butter set around it.

CHICKEN WITH RICE

"age ain' ev'thing: dey's plenty tricks kin swipe him outa sight."

A hen can be most creditably presented thus:

When it has been cleaned and dressed, soak it well in warm water with a little vinegar in it. Then—

A mixture of parsley, thyme, and bay leaf, 2 cloves of garlic, a carrot, and sliced onion into a saucepan where there is water enough to cover your hen. Salt, and pepper, and a red pepper pod. When this has boiled half an hour, it is ready for the entrée of Queen Hen, all cleaned and singed.

In deference to her age, she should be allowed 4 or 5 hours of cooking. 15 minutes before the end, add some well-cooked rice (a cupful raw). Serve it in a deep dish with the chicken and gravy on it.

CANVASBACK DUCK, WITH DELTA DRESSING

"canvasback fly high on de swamp 'cordin' to de wing; but on de table it's 'cordin to his stuffin'."

The most frequent mistake with wild game is overcooking. It should be served quite rare.

2 prs. of canvasback ducks
½ loaf of bread
2 tablespoons of butter
½ cup of celery
1 doz. oysters (small)
1 cup of chopped pecans
Onions, parsley, paprika, salt, pepper, cayenne

Slice crusty bread and toast it, and roll it to crumbs. Wet it, and squeeze it dry. Fry it in the saucepan with chopped onions and celery, adding liberal seasoning and paprika. When it is nearly dry, add the oysters and chopped pecans, which have been slightly toasted.

Stuff the duck with this, and bake it in a hot oven.

"church kin have a good preacher, but if de elders is on'ry, it ain' no 'count; jes lak a dinnah got to have good meat EN' veg'tubles to mek a mark."

STUFFED ARTICHOKES

"arterchoke is lak some folks: got a lot a was'e en' prickles, but w'at's good en em's de bes', ef yo' knows how to get at it."

Boil the artichokes (they should, of course be soaked two or three hours in cold water first for tenderness). While they are still quite hot, take off the top leaves and the 'choke' leaving only several circles of the lower outside leaves. Scrape the 'meat' off the leaves removed. Have ready a little celery, some nuts, and some olives, all very finely chopped, add them to a sauce hollandaise, and pour it over the artichoke. Fold the outer leaves up again to resemble a whole artichoke, and serve hot.

BANANAS

Baked

Bananas   Butter
Sugar

Skin the bananas and clean off the filaments. Brown them in a pan with a little butter and sugar. Put them back in their skins, and set them in the baking dish, attended by much sugar, and a little butter; let them bake moderately for ¾ of an hour or so.

The first browning process will take place quite satisfactorily in lard.

Fried

Bananas   Butter
Sugar

Peel the bananas, skin them and slice them lengthwise. Fry them very slowly till they are quite shriveled and brown as Mandy herself. Drain quickly. Put them in the serving dish and immediately dab a bit of butter on each and sprinkle them well with sugar. Lard is perhaps even better than butter for the frying,—butter is liable to let them burn before they are done.

BUTTER BEANS

A little chopped celery boiled with the butter beans helps them. Drain and put a little butter, or the usual thin roux, and you will see.

SNAP BEANS

"dey allus mekin' a stir 'bout de straw on de back dat camel dat done bus' it; but, lawsy, times things little jes' lak dat wu'ks de yuther way 'roun' fo' de bes'."

The simple snap-bean demands grateful attention for its improvement, if, just before serving, toasted buttered bread crumbs are sprinkled quite lightly over them.

RED BEANS

"costive dish give de po' man pain in de haid to kill joy in de stummick; but raid beans is lak de rain, fo 'rich en' po' alike."

1 quart of red beans
2 quarts of water
1 piece of salt meat, ham, bacon, or pickled pork
1 tablespoon of best lard
1 tablespoon of butter
Carrot, bay leaf, clove of garlic, onion, salt, pepper

Soak the beans 5 or 6 hours, or overnight in cold water. Drain them, and add fresh water, at least 2 qts., to cover them well.

Onions, garlic, carrot, celery, herbs, for flavor. After an hour, the meat. ½ an hour later the lard. They need 2 hours at least on the fire. Add butter just before serving. Rice is its chosen comrade.

One theory holds that the beans are richer in flavor if the preliminary soaking is omitted. In that case, at least 4 hours cooking is essential.

The meat is added after about 2 hours, either whole, or chopped in bits.

BAKED RED BEANS

First the same process as for boiling; but the meat is usually left in one piece, not cut fine. After the boiling, the beans are drained and put in a baking dish, with the meat in the middle. Then fill the dish with the liquid from the boiling process. Put a few strips of sliced bacon across the top. In the oven with it till the liquor is nearly gone,—an hour and a half, about. Boston cannot do better.

BEETS PIQUANTE

2 bunches of beets
3 tablespoons of butter
3 tablespoons of flour
3 tablespoons of vinegar
3 tablespoons of cream
1 tablespoon of sugar
1 cup of hot water
Salt, pepper, cayenne

First, the usual cleaning and boiling. Beets must not be cut, of course, as that causes bleeding and loss of color.
Slice.
Stir the flour in gradually to the melted butter, then thin it by slow addition of hot water, always with stirring. The vinegar, then the cream, finally the sugar and seasoning. and there is a sauce in which you must stir the sliced beets,— to their great advantage.

BRUSSELS SPROUTS AU BEURRE

"cabbages swunk en' gone high sessiety, dat's Brussels sprouts: ain' nothin' in 'em but what's quality."

1 quart of Brussels Sprouts
¼ cup of butter
Celery, salt, pepper, parsley

Clean the sprouts, soak them in cold water, and boil them till they are tender. Just a little celery, minced fine, in the boiling process enhances their flavor.
Put butter in a large saucepan, put in the sprouts with a little chopped parsley, salt, and pepper; give them a good fire and shake them smartly at intervals.
CREAMED—The addition of ¾ cup of milk to the butter in the saucepan just before the sprouts are added produces an agreeable dish, too. A dash of nutmeg should be added for this.

CABBAGE

"fine fedders meks fine birds lak dey sez, en' plain vittles kin hol' dey haid moughty high, come dey got de right fixin'."

Small white cabbage
2 tablespoons of flour
2 tablespoons of butter
1 cup of milk
2 tablespoons of grated American cheese
Salt, pepper, celery salt, chopped parsley

Chop your cabbage,—the small white kind. Quarter it, and immerse it in salted boiling water in an uncovered pot, to boil until tender, then remove to a waiting baking dish.
The saucepan becomes the scene of operations. Melt the butter, stir in the flour carefully, then the milk, stirring always. When it thickens lightly, add the cheese and seasoning.
Pour the sauce over the cabbage in the baking dish, sprinkle it with bread crumbs, and grated cheese and bake until brown. Cauliflower could not be better.

STUFFED CABBAGE

1 medium large white cabbage
1 doz. small sausages, or oysters
½ cup of buttered bread crumbs
1 small piece of ham
1 tablespoon of buter
Onion, ¾ clove of garlic, parsley, red pepper

Quarter the cabbage, tie it in cloth and boil it an hour, take it out and drain it.
For stuffing,—mince the sausage and ham, onions, garlic, and parsley, and put them with the bread crumbs. Fry them all a few minutes in the butter. Open up the cabbage leaves, put in some of the stuffing between them, tie them up again, and give them 2 hours more of baking. Red pepper in the water is worth while.
Pour a cream sauce over it when it is done; it is a hearty meal!

CREOLE CABBAGE

Aunt Melissa is famous for her cabbage; her procedure is simple. First **'gotta take one o' yo' young Creole cabbage, none o' yo' ol' upper country cabbages'**, she says. Tie it in a cloth, and put it in boiling water. Boil 1½ hours. Pour off the water, drain, and pour on more boiling water, adding 1 teaspoon of sugar and 1 teaspoon of salt. Boil in the second water 1½ hours. Drain thoroughly, and serve hot with drawn butter.

CASHAW

Boil the cashaw till it is tender. Then drain it well and cut it in pieces the size of sliced potatoes. Meanwhile, make a simple syrup of sugar and water, and when it thickens, a little, put it in the bottom of the baking dish and set the pieces of cashaw in it. Sprinkle it with a little cinnamon and set it in the oven till the syrup thickens a good deal,—15 minutes should be enough.

CAULIFLOWER BECHAMEL

Cauliflower should be of course soaked 20 minutes head down in cold salt water to get the insects out. Then it is tied up in a cloth and boiled head down,—like a martyr!

Take it out, untie it, set it in a baking dish, and sprinkle it generously with grated Parmesan cheese, then buttered bread crumbs. Bake it, and serve it with yellow Bechamel sauce.

BAKED CELERY

1 large bunch of celery
Buttered bread crumbs
1 cup of thin white sauce
3 tablespoons of grated American cheese
2 tablespoons of chopped red peppers
Salt, pepper, parsley, cayenne

The celery must be chopped in pieces and boiled till it is soft.

Boil some mild red peppers, vein them, and remove the seeds, and chop them. Add 2 tablespoons of them to the celery and put the mixture in a baking dish.

Put the cheese and white sauce together, pour it into the baking dish, and scatter the buttered bread crumbs liberally on top. Bake it a golden brown, and it is a substantial delicacy.

CORN

"two-face in a pusson is a sin; but vegtuhbles de mo' faces dey kin put on, de mo' high yo' gotta reckon 'em."

BAKED CORN VENEZIA

6 ears of corn (2 cups)
3 tablespoons of butter
3 tablespoons of flour
2 cups of milk
1 cup of grated cheese
2 eggs
1 teaspoon of sugar
½ onion, 1 green pepper, salt, pepper

Scrape the ears of corn. Beat the eggs. Remove the veins and seeds from the green pepper, and chop it up,—the onion as well. Cook them in the butter for a few minutes, not letting them brown. Stir in the flour slowly, the milk, then the cheese. Add a good pinch of salt, and the sugar. Finally the corn and eggs.

Put it all in a buttered baking dish, and put a goodly layer of buttered bread

crumbs and grated Parmesan on top. It needs a moderate oven till it is firm, when it is ready for service,—good service!

CREOLE CORN PUDDING

3 eggs
1 pint of milk
4 ears of corn
1 teaspoon of yeast powder
2 teaspoons of butter
Salt, white pepper

Grate the corn, and mix it with the tepid milk. Whip the whole eggs into a froth, and add these, and the other ingredients to the corn and milk. The yeast powder comes last. Bake in a slow oven for 30 or 40 minutes.

CORN FRITTERS

1 can of corn
1 cup of milk
1 tablespoon of butter
1 teaspoon of sugar, salt, pepper.
2 tablespoons of grated cheese
2 eggs

Beat the eggs, and put them with all the other ingredients in a double boiler to cook. It should thicken a good deal,—enough so that it may be molded. A little flour or cracker crumbs may be added at need to bring this about.

When it is thickened, pour it about an inch deep into a large buttered pan. Cut it into strips when it cools, the strips into shorter lengths, and roll them first in egg, then in cracker crumbs, and repeat the process. Fry them in deep fat and drain them. They melt in your mouth.

GRITS (SMALL HOMINY)

"de dress dat ain't fittin' fo' meetin' kin come in handy fo' ev'y day: grits mek no show fo' de comp'ny, but go good in de fam'ly jes' de same."

BOILED GRITS

It must be washed in 2 or 3 waters and drained; then add twice as much water as grits, a good pinch of salt, and let it boil in a double boiler, stirring to avoid lumps.

BAKED

Baking is another form of grits transmutation: stir up the cold cooked grits with a cup of milk (more or less according to the quantity of grits), add a beaten egg, with pepper and salt; put the mixture in the oven to bake.

FRIED GRITS

The left-over hot grits must be smoothed evenly in a platter. For another meal, it can reappear most acceptably, fried. Slice the cold grits. Beat up an egg and season it with salt and pepper. Dip the sliced grits in it, then in flour, or cracker crumbs; repeat that process, and then fry the slices in deep hot grease.

EGG-PLANT

Peel egg-plants, dice them, or cube them, or cut them in thin slivers; sprinkle the pieces with salt and let them be for 15 minutes or more. Dip them in egg, then in crumbs, or simply in a batter, and drop them in deep hot grease to fry. Drain them. They are crisp and crunchy.

EGGPLANT
STUFFED WITH SHRIMP

"put a little bit o' ev'ything yo' has, wid somep'n good to weigh it down, en' yo' got a good stuffin'."

1 large eggplant
1 cup of buttered bread crumbs
1 tablespoon of butter
1 lb. of shrimp
2 onions, 1 clove of garlic, green pepper, parsley salt, pepper

Boil the eggplant; then peel it, cutting the peeling in large shapely pieces, and putting them aside. Mash the pulp. Have the shrimp peeled and chopped.

Assail the onion, garlic, et cet., with the chopping knife; fry the pieces in butter a little, until they are browned.

Add the shrimp, the mashed pulp, the bread crumbs, and mix them up well. Fill the pieces of eggplant skin with the mixture. Sprinkle some bread crumbs on top of each, and give them 15 minutes in a moderate oven.

If you do not favor shrimp, increase the quantity of bread crumbs a little, and add a little chopped ham, or bacon, or sausage.

MIRLETON

Vegetable pears, otherwise known as mirleton, can be treated exactly like egg-plant or squash, i. e., fried, or stuffed with the same sort of stuffing. It has a flavor all its own, worth knowing.

KUSH-KUSH

"good on de tongue en' easy on de stumick, da's how to cook fo' chilluns."

2 cups of cornmeal
½ cup of hot water
2 cups of milk
1 egg
¾ teaspoon of baking powder
1 teaspoon of sugar (or syrup), salt

Scald the cornmeal in hot water, then stir the milk into it, then the beaten egg, and the sugar. Add the salt and baking powder.

Have the skillet very hot, then lower the fire, and put the mixture in the skillet to cook over a moderate flame. Stir it often, and let it cook till it is well browned. Children love it for breakfast.

MUSTARD GREENS

They are cooked like spinach,—a good flavor, but not quite so delicate.

OKRA

Okra, like mushrooms, is fastidious; it must be cooked in a porcelain-lined or agate pan, otherwise it turns black.

BOILED OKRA

Wash the okra and pare the ends. Cook it in boiling salt water about 20 minutes. Drain it well, and serve with drawn butter.

STEWED OKRA AND TOMATOES

1 quart of okra
1 tablespoon of butter
3 tomatoes
Onion, green pepper, parsley, garlic, salt, pepper, cayenne, liberal seasoning

Prepare the okra by washing it and paring the ends.

Let the chopped up onion, sweet pepper, and garlic, simmer in the butter several minutes. Then add the chopped tomatoes and their juice with the okra, and let it all cook together.

LETTUCE AU JUS

4 small heads of iceberg lettuce
2 tablespoons of butter
1 tablespoon of flour
1 cup of water (or soup stock)
Salt, pepper, parsley, thyme, bay leaf, green pepper

Take off the outside leaves; clean the lettuce well, and let them cook 20 minutes in boiling water. Take them out, dip them in cold water, and let them drain on a cloth.

Melt the butter, and make a roux with the flour letting it brown a little. Then add the water and seasonings, and the lettuces. Let them cook an hour basting often. Serve them in a deep dish with the sauce poured over them.

ONIONS

"dey's good, en' bad, en' better, en' wuzzer; but ain' many gotta-be's. Onions is one o' 'em."

CREAMED ONIONS POINTE COUPEE

Medium sized onions
Thick cream sauce
Parsley, paprika, salt, pepper

Leave the onions in boiling salt water until they are tender. Drain them well, and pour cream sauce over them, sprinkling chopped parsley and paprika over the top.

They are effective served on individual rounds of toast, set on a flat dish with the cream sauce poured over them. A cheese sauce is very good with them too; or even simply drawn butter.

FRENCH FRIED ONIONS

Onions
Milk
Flour
Lard

Slice the onions very thin, cut them in slivers like French fried potatoes, and soak them in ice-water for some time, then drain them and dry them well. A milk bath of 15 minutes, then drain them again, dip them in flour and fry them in deep fat. Drain them on butcher's paper and sprinkle them with salt. They are a perfect touch with steak or liver.

POTATOES BONHOMME

Operations begin with potatoes baked in their clean jackets. Slit them down one side, scoop out the contents, and mash it up with cream, onion juice, salt, pepper, butter, cayenne, a little paprika, and bits of crisp bacon. Stuff the jackets with this, put a bit of bacon over the slit, and a dab of butter and paprika. Run them back in the oven for a few minutes, and serve.

POTATO ROSE RING

A potato ring is an effective frame, for fish particularly. Mashed potatoes, stiffer than the usual consistency for serving, are put in a pastry bag, and by use of a star-tube forced through with the shape of a rose. Mix the yolk of an egg with a little water and brush the potatoes with a little of the mixture, run the potatoes in the oven a moment, and serve.

POTATOES SOUFFLES

This is a French heritage direct, for which New Orleans restaurants are famous. It is easy, but tricky,—success is worth while.

Use old potatoes. Slice them as thick as a silver dollar, and soak them in ice-water. Cook them in only moderately hot grease till they begin to brown slightly, then take then out, let them cool a moment, and pop them into sizzling deep grease. Fish them out, drain them, sprinkle them with salt, and serve instantly. They are a credit to you. Do not put in too many at once in the last grease: crowding will keep them from swelling.

SWEET POTATOES

"costive en' good looks de same ter some folks; but Lawsy, take a yaller yam: don' cos' nothin', en' tas'e a heap."

FRIED SWEET POTATOES

Raw sweet potatoes, sliced and fried in deep lard, like Irish potatoes, are good. A little salt is sprinkled on them when they are done, then they are just touched with butter, and, if desired, very lightly sprinkled with sugar. Cold baked sweet potatoes, cut in thick slices, fried in butter sprinkled with a little sugar are very good.

YAMS LOUISIANE

2 large yams
Sugar
Butter
½ cup of water

Boil the sweet potatoes, slice them thickly; put a layer of them in the bottom of a baking dish; sprinkle thickly with sugar and put liberal dabs of butter about; another layer of potatoes, and again, sugar and butter, repeat till the dish is full, finishing with sugar and butter. Add a dash of cinnamon. Pour the water over all and bake it in a slow oven.

CANDIED YAMS

Boil the sweet potatoes, peel and slice them rather thick, or quarter them lengthwise. Make a syrup of sugar and water, and when it thickens slightly, cover the bottom of a baking pan with it. Put in the sliced potatoes, and cook them in a slow oven till the syrup is nearly candied. A little cinnamon is good with them.

An extra touch much in favor is to sprinkle some raisins or pecans, or both, in with the yams. Also marshmallows may be set on top, just a few minutes before it is time to take the dish from the oven.

BAKED SWEET POTATOES

Boiled sweet potatoes mashed up well with liberal butter and sugar, a touch of cinnamon, and the juice of a lemon are put in a baking dish, with a sprinkling of sugar and a few dabs of butter on top. Steam for ½ an hour.

SWEET POTATO CROQUETTES

Boil the potatoes and mash them up with liberal butter, a very little sugar, till they are of a pliable consistency. Work in with them some crisp chopped pecans; mold them into small cylinders, or flat croquettes and brown them in butter.

PLANTAINS

Plantains are like heavy bananas, not sweet, and good only for cooking. They are firmer, but less delicate than bananas. They must be blackish to be ripe. They are prepared like bananas, but need longer cooking.

SWEET PEPPERS

"mighty little en' mighty little kin mek a lot when dey gets tergedder: put mos' ennything in er pepper, en' yo' got a dish full o' quality."

Peppers, like eggplants, squash, and mirleton, are used with various stuffings. They must be parboiled and have the veins and seeds removed, and the stems cut flat always. Bread crumbs, with rice and corn are favorite stuffings, and always a bit of ham or bacon, or sausage, for seasoning. The same shrimp stuffing suggested for eggplants is excellent with peppers.

PEPPERS AU MAIS

6 peppers
½ cup of bread crumbs
1 cup of corn
¼ cup of cream
1 egg
Grated ham
Salt, pepper, paprika, cayenne, parsley

The peppers are scalded for a few minutes, and seeds and veins removed.

Mix all the ingredients together and fill the peppers with the mixture. Sprinkle a few bread crumbs and some bits of breakfast bacon on top.

Cover the bottom of a baking pan with water, and set the peppers in it to cook for ½ an hour. Have an eye to them and baste them during the time.

PEPPERS A L'ITALIEN

6 sweet peppers
1½ cups of boiled rice
1 cup of canned tomatoes
4 tablespoons of cream
½ cup of bread crumbs
½ cup of walnuts (Eng.)
Bit of ham
Parsley, onion, salt, pepper, cayenne, paprika

Prepare the peppers, scalding, removing veins and seeds. Mix the various ingredients,—a thick tomato puree may replace the tomatoes and cream, to advantage. Fill the peppers with the mixture. Sprinkle bread crumbs on each pepper; bits of bacon, too, are good.

Put them in the baking pan, with just a bit of water to keep them from burning, and let them brown.

BOILED RICE

The ideal is for each grain to be white, and separate, and well-cooked. Wash the rice thoroughly.

Put it slowly into enough boiling salted water to cover it well, and let it boil busily for about 20 minutes. Then it goes into the colander, to have cold water run through it thoroughly. Set the colander over boiling water for 2 hours. Just before serving, run it for a moment into the oven.

It is good with butter, with gravies, with milk and sugar,—essential in gumbo.

PILAFF

A cup of rice, mixed with cooked tomatoes that have run through a colander,—salt, pepper, chopped onions, and you have a pilaff, delicious with fricassee of chicken, or with grillades.

For JAMBALAYA, see Entrées.

SQUASH—FRIED

Slice the squash across, very thin, set the slices in salt water, then wipe them dry. Sprinkle them with salt and pepper; dip them first in flour, then in egg, then in cracker crumbs, and repeat that process several times. Then into deep hot fat with them, for frying. When they are done, drain them on butcher's paper, and they are delicious.

STUFFED SQUASH

Any of the stuffings recommended for eggplants and sweet peppers are equally good with squash. Also, it can be boiled, the contents scraped out and mixed with buttered bread crumbs, a little chopped pepper (sweet), onion, and salt, put back and baked until brown.

SPINACH

"dey sez spinach is ez good es a doctor; huh, it's better'n dat, 'cause it don' leave no bills trailin'."

BAKED SPINACH

2 bunches of spinach
2 tablespoons of flour
1 egg
1 cup of milk
1 tablespoon of butter
½ cup of bread crumbs
Sherry flavoring
Salt, pepper, cayenne

Clean the spinach, and boil it quite thoroughly.

Make a roux, adding the flour slowly to the butter; then beat in the egg and milk, add the seasoning and sherry flavoring. Beat all of this with the spinach. Put it in a buttered baking dish, sprinkle bread crumbs on top and consign it to a moderate oven. Sliced hard-boiled eggs should garnish it for serving.

Instead of using sherry flavoring, and the roux named, a rich cheese sauce may be used instead, and grated cheese mixed with the bread and crumbs to sprinkle over the top.

SPINACH RAMEKINS

1 cup of chopped spinach
2 eggs
Salt, pepper, paprika
Cheese sauce

Clean and boil the spinach, chop it up and beat it well with the eggs. Put the mixture into buttered custard cups; set them in water and let them cook at moderate heat till they begin to get firm. Serve them with a cheese sauce.

TOMATOES

"sometimes dey's one answer to a askin', en' den again dey's two, en' den times dey's plenty; but when it comes ter how can yo' cook up tomatoes, dey jes' nach'ly ain' no end o' em."

FRIED TOMATOES

The tomatoes must not be very ripe,—quite firm. Make a thin batter of flour with egg, salt, pepper, and cayenne in it; dip the slices of tomato in it, and fry them in deep grease.

TOMATOES JEANNETTE

Slice large firm tomatoes. Round thin slices of bread and toast them. Put a slice of tomato on each slice of toast; sprinkle them thickly with salt, pepper, cayenne, lots of grated cheese, and paprika. Into the oven for a moderate baking.

TOMATOES DE LUXE

Hollow out large, firm tomatoes, put an egg in each one; sprinkle them well with salt, pepper, and grated cheese; put 2 strips of bacon across the top. 20 minutes in a moderate oven, and the good culinary deed is done. A tomato sauce may be served with them.

STUFFED TOMATOES WITH SPINACH

Boiled spinach well chopped, mixed with a little cream sauce, or cheese sauce makes a delicious stuffing for tomatoes. Sprinkle a few bread crumbs over the top, and let them spend 15 minutes in a moderate oven.

TOMATOES VENEZIA

2 cups of canned tomatoes
1 cup of bread crumbs
½ cup of grated cheese
½ tablespoon of butter
1 onion, parsley, salt, pepper, cayenne.

Use the pulp of the canned tomatoes, not the juice, in measuring your cupfuls.

Chop up the onions and parsley mix them with all the other ingredients, and with lavish seasoning.

Pour it all into a buttered baking dish, and sprinkle a heavy shower of bread crumbs and grated cheese on top. Then give it 20 minutes in a hot oven.

TURNIPS

A few potatoes mashed up with the turnips improve their flavor.

TOMATOES A L'ESPAGNOL

Firm tomatoes
Green peppers
Butter
Sugar
Onion, garlic, salt, pepper

Cut the tomatoes crosswise in half. Season each with salt and pepper, and cayenne, and rub a little garlic across each half. Sprinkle a little sugar over them. Pour a little melted butter over each piece, cover it thickly with green peppers chopped small, with a small dab of butter cn top. Put them in a buttered baking dish (glass or porcelain lined) and bake them till they are soft,—about 20 minutes.

SAUCES

"vittles good deyselves, da's one thing; keepin' comp'ny tergedder good, da's ernudder. Take de bofe, en' it's good eatin'."

WHITE SAUCE

This classic is so well known it hardly needs repetition:

2 tablespoons of butter
1½ tablespoons of flour
1 cup of scalded milk
Salt, pepper

Let the butter melt and bubble on a slow fire; stir the flour into it with care,—also with salt and pepper! Then the milk, very, very slowly, stirred, and 2 minutes of boiling.

WHITE SAUCE PARISIENNE

Start as above with butter, flour, and seasoning. BUT—have ready the yolk of an egg, beaten up with a little vinegar. When the flour and butter are creamy smooth, stir in a cup of water; then take the sauce off, add the beaten yolk, and set where it will be warm, but not boil.

DRAWN BUTTER SAUCE

2 heaping tablespoons of butter
2 tablespoons of flour
Salt, pepper
1 cup of boiling water

Melt 1 tablespoon of butter, then stir in the flour, with the salt and pepper in it, smoothly. Very little by very little, add the water, always stirring. Take the sauce off the fire, and add the other butter, in small bits, still with stirring.

EGG SAUCE FOR FISH

Sliced or chopped hard-boiled eggs added to drawn butter sauce are perfect accompaniment for fish.

EGG SAUCE

Drawn butter sauce develops into egg sauce, when the yolks of 2 eggs are beaten into it, and a little lemon juice added.

SAUCE PIQUANTE

Melted butter, lemon juice, French mustard, a dash of paprika, and very finely chopped parsley.

BROWN ROUX

2 tablespoons of butter
1 tablespoon of flour
1 glass of water
Salt, pepper

Stir the flour with the seasoning into the melted butter, and when it is smooth and the butter brown add the boiling water, stirring slowly. You may use more flour and water, if the number of guests require it. This is a substantial base, for Sauce Piquante Parisienne.

SAUCE PIQUANTE PARISIENNE

Brown Roux
1 tablespoon of butter
3 tablespoons of vinegar
3 or 4 pickles
Shallot tops, parsley, salt, pepper

Have ready your brown roux (described above). Mince the shallot tops and parsley, and put them in a saucepan over a slow fire, with the butter and vinegar. When the butter has melted add the brown roux, and chopped pickles.

WHITE ROUX

White Roux is the same as Brown Roux, except that the butter is not allowed to brown.

CAPER SAUCE

As simple as arithmetic: Drawn Butter sauce, plus ½ cup or more of capers drained of their juice.

CAPER SAUCE PARISIENNE

Look back at White Sauce Parisienne: follow the same steps, except that you omit the vinegar, and add capers when ready to serve. Nice with a boiled fish.

SAUCE ITALIENNE

Parsley, shallot tops, mushrooms, garlic
1 cup of cooking wine
Salt, pepper
1 teaspoon of olive oil
1 teaspoon of butter

Chop the parsley, shallots, mushrooms, and garlic well, and let them cook on a slow fire 20 minutes with the wine. Add salt, and pepper, and the oil. When ready to serve, stir in the butter rubbed into a little flour.

SAUCE HOLLANDAISE

"how long en' how hot matters much ez whut yo' puts in."

½ cup of butter
2 eggs
¾ teaspoon of lemon juice
¼ cup of thin cream (or water)
Salt, cayenne

Wash the butter in ice-water to remove the salt, and work it until it is soft.

To ⅓ of the butter, add the yolks and lemon juice, and put them in a saucepan set in a larger one containing hot water. Stir with a wooden spoon until the butter and eggs are blended. Stir and stir and add the remainder of the butter very slowly, stirring continually.

When it has thickened well, add slowly the hot thin cream (or water) the salt and cayenne.

WARNING: beware of curdling. Two things count,—adding the butter very slowly, and watching the water in the lower pan, which must simmer only, not boil.

SAUCE BEARNAISE

This is much like Hollandaise; but instead of the lemon juice, use tarragon vinegar and 1 teaspoon each of parsley, capers, and (if possible) fresh tarragon, finely chopped.

TARTAR SAUCE

Mayonnaise with mustard in it, and a few finely chopped pickles and capers, makes an acceptable tartar sauce.

SAUCE RAVIGOTE

"put somp'n good to somp'n good, en' yo' boun' ter git somp'n better, ef yo' do it right."

Parsley, water cress, estragon, and a bit of garlic mashed well together begin this, crushed into a little cake. Beat in with a wooden spoon the raw yolk of an egg, and add olive oil drop by drop. When it is properly thick, add a little vinegar and mustard. This is delicious with cold beef or brisket.

POULETTE SAUCE

Very like its cousin Blanquette following; but before serving, have the yolk of an egg (well separated from the white) beaten up first with a little water, then with a little of the sauce. Add it to Sauce Blanquette.

SAUCE BLANQUETTE

1 tablespoon of butter
1 tablespoon of flour
1 cup of water
Parsley, salt, pepper

Melt the butter, then stir in the flour very slowly, add the water, salt, pepper, and chopped parsley. Simple and good for veal and chicken.

SAUCE POYDRAS

5 tablespoons of tomato catsup
4 teaspoons of a smooth French mustard (not the hot)
½ teaspoon of brown onion juice
2 teaspoons of Worcestershire sauce
Paprika, salt

This is very good with cold roast or brisket.
Note: For directions for making a smooth French mustard look under salads.

ITALIAN SAUCE FOR SPAGHETTI

½ cup of olive oil
1 can of tomato paste
3 cloves of garlic, salt, pepper

Fry the garlic in the olive oil till it is quite yellow. Then mix the tomato paste with an equal amount of water, and add to the olive oil and garlic. Let it simmer until thick, then add salt and pepper. Grated Parmesan cheese, must be sprinkled on the spaghetti with this.

SOUTHERN SAUCE

Peel 2 pieces of garlic; mash them into a cake, then add the yolk of a raw egg, and a little piece of the inside of the bread, dipped in milk; then salt and pepper.

Mix these well together, then stir in olive oil, drop by drop, as in making mayonnaise. This is delicious with cold beef, muton, or fowl.

SAUCE TOMATE
(FOR CROQUETTES)

¼ cup of butter
⅓ cup of flour
1½ cups of brown stock
1½ cups of tomato pulp (stewed and strained)
Slice of carrot, of onion, 2 cloves, bay leaf, parsley, salt, pepper, tabasco

Brown the butter and flour together, stirring constantly. When well-mixed and smooth, add the stock and tomato pulp, and herbs. Let it simmer for 10 minutes, and add salt, pepper, and tabasco.

"wouldn't be no trouble 'bout salvation ef ev'ybody 'd give in ter grace lak salad does ter fixin'."

Our French inheritance is in evidence in our attitude towards salads. The taste that feels a fine careless rapture in mad minglings of bananas and cheeses and nuts and pickles, finds cool response here. Paris, which does such marvels with hors d'oeuvres uses lettuce almost uniquely as its salad, 'mariné' (saturated) in simple dressings. However, we have some few developments.

FRENCH DRESSING

Twice as much oil as vinegar; salt, pepper, cayenne, paprika; a good dash of Creole mustard, put in with this a quartered onion and a whole clove of garlic, and let it soak for days. When it is served, it is poured off the onion and garlic. Mandy always has a bottle of this in the ice box, and it has always been soaking a week before she allows it to be used. It should be very cold, just out of the ice box.

CREOLE MUSTARD

Make a paste of powdered English mustard and warm water. Then beat olive oil into it very, very slowly. When it has taken up all the oil possible, add vinegar, a little sugar and salt to taste.

SAUCE REMOULADE

Chop up water cress, parsley, a tiny bit of garlic, a bit of onion, as finely as possible. Then mash it all to a pulp. Add a tablespoon of powdered mustard to this, and beat olive oil into it drop by drop, beating with all possible vigor, and adding the oil till there is a sauce of moderate consistency. Then add a little vinegar, pepper, and salt.

THOUSAND ISLAND DRESSING

½ cup of mayonnaise
1 cup of Chili sauce
Green onion tops, green peppers, salt, pepper, paprika chopped

Beat all of this together well, till it is thoroughly mixed. Add a little olive oil, and beat again.

ROQUEFORT CHEESE DRESSING

Mash up Roquefort cheese well, and beat it into a highly seasoned French dressing.

MAYONNAISE CREOLE DRESSING

3 eggs (yolks)
1 lemon (the juice)
1½ tablespoons of sugar
1¾ cups of olive oil
Salt, cayenne

Beat the oil into the eggs very, very slowly. Add the seasonings, beating all the while. Set in the ice box.

FRUIT SALAD DRESSING

2 eggs
2 tablespoons of butter
4 tablespoons of lemon juice
Salt, pepper, paprika

Beat up the eggs well, yolks and whites together. Put the lemon juice in the double-boiler and when it is hot add the eggs. When it gets creamy take it off and add the butter, salt, pepper, and paprika liberally.

SALAD PAYSAN

"cabbage haid ha'd in de ga'den, but mek moughty sof' eatin' at de table."

1 cup of chopped cabbage (hard white)
1 cup of celery
½ cup of chopped pimentos
½ cup of vinegar
2 green peppers, green onion tops
Salt, pepper
¼ cup of sugar
½ package of gelatine

Chop all of the ingredients very fine, particularly the cabbage. Mix them all together and put in the seasoning. Have the gelatine soaking in cold water and add the mixture to it, and pour it all together into a wet ring mold.

It is pretty and dainty to see,—and even better to eat,—garnished with lettuce, and served with mayonnaise in the center.

SALAD MARINEE

Head of lettuce
½ cup of vinegar
1 teaspoon each of chopped onion and
    parsley, green peppers, and any
    herbs.
Button mushrooms
Pimentos
Salt, white pepper, paprika

Soak the herbs at least an hour in the vinegar. Estragon, if available, is very desirable, with them. Strain them, and add seasoning.

Have the lettuce well washed, and wrapped in muslin salad bag on the ice. Take it out, arrange it in the salad bowl with pimentos and mushrooms, pour the dressing over it, and toss it lightly till well covered with dressing. Then add olive oil, and continue to toss lightly, till the olive oil is well through it. The usual method of mixing the oil and vinegar lessens the spiced vinegar's permeation, they say. Estragon chopped finely over the dish is good in moderation.

The procedure is good even omitting the mushrooms and pimentos. This ritual is essentially French.

ASPARAGUS TIPS

Asparagus tips make a delicious salad, garnished with lettuce, and ringed with sliced green pepper, and a little paprika sprinkled over them. The following is a good dressing for them: First put salt in the oil; then stir the vinegar slowly into the oil, using twice as much oil as vinegar. Then a good dash of Creole mustard; onion juice (or scraped onion). Add tomato ketchup, equal to the quantity of oil and vinegar, then a touch of Worcestershire, tabasco and cayenne. It must be very highly and hotly seasoned.

CRAB SALAD

1 lb. of crab meat
1 small bottle of sweet pickles
2 hard-boiled eggs
Mayonnaise
Salt, pepper, paprika

Use white crab meat. Chop up the eggs and pickles not too fine. Mix them up with the crab meat. Add the seasoning liberally. Put in at least as much mayonnaise as there is of the other ingredients,—preferably more. Put in a freezer, pack with ice, and let it stand several hours. Serve with mayonnaise.

BEET SALAD CELESTE

"de tongue en' de eye is close frien's: yo' please one, it he'p pleasin' de yuther."

2 bunches of beets
½ cup of cream
Mayonnaise
1 box of gelatine

Boil the beets in the usual manner, having them thoroughly cooked and tender. Mash them through a colander, add the cream and as much mayonnaise, salt, and pepper, to taste.

Have the gelatine soaking in cold water, and add the beet mixture to it and pour it in a ring mold.

It is a most effective dish, served with lettuce as garnish, the center of the ring filled with mayonnaise,—very gay in color.

"alligatah pear lak salvation: good any way it come."

ALLIGATOR PEAR

Alligator pear is a monarch of salads. It is delicious, served simply with French dressing. Or chopped up with quartered tomatoes, and green peppers.

Or it can be served with sliced oranges, the oranges heaped in the center, the alligator pear, cut in large pieces, outlining them, and a rather tart French dressing poured over it all.

AVOCADO HENRI

Alligator pear (avocado)
Boiled shrimp
Celery
1 small bottle of olives stuffed with
    pimentos
Green pepper, cayenne,
Anchovies

This is so rich that it far oversteps its obligations as a salad course.

The alligator pears are halved, and skinned, the seed, of course, removed.

Mince up the shrimp very, very finely; chop up the celery and stuffed olives, the green pepper, and if you wish, a little anchovy, mix them with the shrimp, and make it all into a paste by adding mayonnaise. Spread the mayonnaise smoothly, like an icing, over the top, and cross anchovies over it. A matchless dish.

The anchovies may be omitted, of course, in which case, slices of the stuffed olives arranged on top are effective.

Asparagus may take the place of shrimp, if you prefer.

salads and dressings

ALLIGATOR PEAR VALCOUR

Very ripe alligator pears, please. Press them through a colander. Mix with them chopped stuffed olives, chopped celery, and some mayonnaise. Pack it all in a mold; freeze it, and serve it sliced with more mayonnaise over it. It is a meal in itself,—and such a meal!

SHRIMP FRAPPE

2 lbs. of shrimp
1 package of gelatine
½ cup of cold water
1½ cups of hot water
1 can of tomatoes
4 hard-boiled eggs
1 tablespoon of vinegar
2 teaspoons each of sugar and salt
Onion, salt, pepper, celery, cayenne, parsley

Chop up the onion, and boil it with the tomatoes, vinegar, sugar, salt, and seasoning, in 1½ cups of water.

Let the gelatine soak for several minutes in the cold water. Take the boiling mixture from the fire and pour it over the gelatine.

Chop up the boiled shrimp, celery, egg, parsley together, fill a mold, or individual molds, with the mixture, then pour the liquid over it. Set it in the ice box and when it congeals, bring it out and enjoy it.

STUFFED TOMATOES

6 tomatoes
¾ lb. of chopped nuts
3 tablespoons of mayonnaise
1 tablespoon of gelatine
Salt, pepper, cayenne, celery

Choose nicely shaped firm tomatoes. Cut the tops off and hollow the tomatoes. Chop up the nuts and celery with the scooped out 'meat' of the tomato, add the juice, too, and the mayonnaise.

Dissolve the gelatine in cold water add it to the mixture, and set it on ice. As it begins to harden, fill the tomatoes with it, and put additional mayonnaise and chopped green pepper on top. The tomatoes should be well chilled.

GRAPEFRUIT SALAD

Grapefruit peeled, and the sections carefully skinned whole, makes an effective looking salad, served on lettuce leaves. It should be sprinkled with paprika, and a good French dressing poured over it.

ARTICHOKE SALAD FRAPPE

"ev'y thing got its high en' low: salad cain' reach pas' dis-yeah."

10 artichokes
2 cups of water
3 teaspoons of gelatine
Salt, pepper, cayenne
Mayonnaise

This is a favorite salad of a family renowned for its cuisine.

Soak the artichokes long in cold water; boil them, drain them, and take off the leaves. Leave the hearts whole, scrape the 'meat' from the tips of the leaves, and add about ¾ of a cup of mayonnaise, with seasoning liberally.

Dissolve the gelatine in the water, and add this to the mixture, stirring it all together well and pour it into a mold.

Arrange the 8 whole hearts in this, and set the mold in the ice box to harden.

It is not so difficult as it sounds, and is more delicious. It is particularly effective when served in a ring mold with mayonnaise in the center and lettuce leaves around, with slices of red tomatoes on them.

STUFFED ARTICHOKE

Boil the artichokes, after having soaked them several hours in cold water, as usual. While they are still quite hot, remove the upper leaves and the choke; leaving only a few lower circles of leaves. Mix together mayonnaise, with much finely chopped celery, stuffed olives, and nuts. Scrape the 'meat' from the leaves removed and add this. Open up the leaves on the artichoke, and put this filling in; then close the leaves once more, to resemble a whole artichoke; hold them in place with a cord. Set them in the ice box, till ready to serve. Then remove the cord and bring them on.

WALDORF SALAD

Celery
Nuts
Apples
Mayonnaise
Cheese

Two parts of celery, about, to one each of apples, and nuts. They must all be chopped very fine, well-seasoned with salt, pepper, and paprika. Mix a little mayonnaise with them, and sprinkle grated cheese over it. It can be served on lettuce; an apple or orange basket may be used as a container.

CELERY SQUARES

Celery makes a delicious salad, with a sauce remoulade. It should be well cleaned, and the green leaves taken off; then cut it in small squares and serve it on lettuce leaves. The green leaves may be used chopped up in the sauce.

VEGETABLE SALAD

Left over string beans, or butter beans, even, are delicious, served on lettuce, with a French dressing poured over them. Quartered tomatoes may be served with them. Peas, carrots, cauliflower, may be used in the same way.

"dey talks erbout a sweet toof lak dey's on'y one; huh! by de end o' dinnah dey's all o' 'em sweet."

MERINGUE DESSERT

6 whites of eggs
2 cups of sugar
¼ teaspoon of salt
1 teaspoon of vanilla
1 teaspoon of vinegar
Whipped cream

Beat the whites as stiff as possible. Add the sugar gradually, then in turn the salt, vanilla and vinegar.

Grease 2 pans with butter, pour in the mixture and bake in a moderate oven about 45 minutes. Cut in squares.

Cover ½ of the squares with whipped cream, with preserves or fruit on top,—this is filling, over which must be placed the other squares,, which again have whipped cream heaped over them with a touch of preserves or fruit. Very chic, this.

PEACH MERINGUE

1½ cups of peaches (canned or fresh)
1 cup of sugar
2 cups of milk
3 eggs.

Line a mold with lady-fingers and put the peaches in.

Stir together the sugar and milk and eggs, and pour the mixture over the peaches. Let it stand a while, then put it in the oven.

Take it out and put it on ice, with a meringue.

HAWAIIAN SWEET

1 apple, orange, banana, pineapple, cherries
1 cup of pecans
1 doz. marshmallows (quartered)
½ pint of cream
1 heaping tablespoon of gelatine
1 teaspoon of vanilla
2 tablespoons of sugar

Cut up the fruit and the pecans and put them all together with the quartered marshmallows. Put the sugar in the cream and add the vanilla. The gelatine must be dissolved in the slightly heated pineapple juice, and added to the other ingredients. Set it all in a mold, in a cool place.

CREME AU CHOCOLAT

1 pint of milk
6 tablespoons of sugar
2 bars of chocolate
3 eggs

Put the sugar in the milk and set it on the fire; when it comes to a boil, take it off.

Have the chocolate grated and add to it 2 tablespoons of the sugared milk, stir it till it is well melted, then add the rest of the milk and set it to cool.

Into the milk beat the yellows of 3 eggs and 1 white, then strain it, pour it into individual custard dishes, (or a big custard dish) and set in a pan of water. Bake 15 or 20 minutes in a moderate oven.

VANILLA may be used as flavoring, instead of chocolate. Or COFFEE; or ORANGE-FLOWER WATER, 1 teaspoonful.

BEIGNETS DE POMMES

"apple mek heap o' trouble 'roun' Eden; but he sho' bin makin' up fo' it sence."

2 cups of flour
2 eggs
1 tablespoon of brandy (or 2 of cooking wine)
1 cup of milk
4 apples

Put the flour in a deep bowl, and make a little hollow in the center of it. in which you must put the beaten yellows of the eggs and the rum (or wine).

Slow is the word. Stir the flour into the eggs slowly, add the milk, very slowly, stirring constantly. Have the whites of the eggs beaten, and stir them in,—slowly!

Core firm cooking apples and slice them thin, dip each slice in the batter and fry it in very hot lard, or butter. Sprinkle with powdered sugar, and serve to guests, who will at once think of Paris.

Peaches, apricots, and strawberries (these last whole and large) may be used in the same way.

ZABAGLIONE

6 eggs
¼ cup of sugar
1 cup of rum (or cooking wine)

Beat up the yellows of the eggs with the sugar and the rum, and put the mixture in a double boiler. Let it cook to a thick cream stirring the while with a wooden spoon. Beat with vim the whites of eggs. When the cream has thickened take it off and add the whites at once, beating vigorously. Serve at once, to the joy of all.

If wine is used instead of rum, add a pinch of cinnamon, and hope for better luck next time!

APPLES AUX CROUTES

Apples
Sugar
Bread
Butter

Peel and core the apples. Cut slices of bread in rounds about the size of the apples. In the baking dish put the rounds of bread, an apple on each. Powdered sugar and liberal dabs of butter must fill the apple centers. Put them in a very moderate oven, baste them frequently, and add more sugar and dabs of butter.

Serve on the bread, with the sauce from the baking pan poured over them, and a bit of preserves in the center, if you will.

Easy, wholesome, and delectable.

APPLE FONDU

Apples
Nuts
Raisins
Sugar
Whipped cream

Peel and core the apples. Fill each center with nuts and raisins, the raisins on top.

Set the apples in a baking pan, the bottom of which is covered with water, and sprinkle sugar thickly over it all. Cook in a very slow oven with frequent and attentive bastings. It appears at the table surmounted with whipped cream, and tasting very rich. The water will have become a thick syrup. It is well to have them cooked several hours before they are to be served.

APPLES WITH RICE

1 cup of rice
½ pint of milk
8 apples
1 egg
4 tablespoons of sugar

Cook the rice thoroughly in the milk, stirring it with 2 tablespoons of sugar.

Peel and core 4 apples and put them in a baking pan, the bottom of which is covered with water, sweetened with 2 tablespoons of sugar, or more.

Cook the apples slowly until they are tender, then take them off and drain them.

The other 4 apples are peeled, cored, and chopped in pieces. Cook them now in the syrup from the baked apples, adding a little grated lemon peel, till they make a sauce. Then stir in the rice and let it cool a ¼ of an hour. Then stir in the beaten yellow of an egg.

Set the baked apples in a baking dish, pour the sauce around them, leaving only the tops exposed, and leave them in the oven till they brown a little. Fill the centers of the apples with preserves, and serve them in the midst of their rice-sauce surroundings. This, too, is O, so French!

STRAWBERRY SHORT CAKE (Sweet)

4 eggs
1 cup of sugar
¾ of a cup of matzos flour
1 quart of berries
1 pint of whipping cream
Salt, lemon rind

The berries are washed, picked, halved, sprinkled thickly with sugar and left in peace for 2 or 3 hours.

Beat the eggs and sugar together well, add a good pinch of salt and a little grated lemon peel. Sift in the flour and mix it well; bake this batter in shallow cake tins.

When ready to serve, the berries are put in as fillers between the cakes with some of their juice and liberal whipped cream, and the top 'iced' in the same manner.

Ordinary biscuit dough, rather short and rolled very thin, makes a delicious short cake. It is cooked in shallow pans, with a filling and icing of the sweetened whipped cream and berries. Many prefer it to the sweeter cake.

CHOCOLATE MOUSSE

"quick-come comp'ny in de parlor need quick hand in de kitchen."

4 eggs (whites)
6 tablespoons of powdered sugar
2 squares of chocolate

Beat up the eggs well, beat in the sugar gradually, and, very gradually, the grated chocolate. A little whipped cream may be used with the whites of the eggs if desired.

STRAWBERRY MOUSSE

1 quart of berries
1 pint of cream
Powdered sugar

Pick, wash, and halve the berries, cover them with powdered sugar, and let them be an hour or two. Then strain them.

Whip the cream, mix it with the berries and a little of the juice. It is delicious, frozen.

PEACH or MACAROONS may be used with the whipped cream, instead of strawberries.

PRUNE WHIP

1 lb. of prunes
1 cup of sugar
1 lemon
4 eggs
1 cup of chopped nuts
Whipped cream

An hour's soaking for the prunes, then boil them an hour. Mash them up well and add a cup of sugar.

Strain, and add the lemon juice, and a little grated lemon peel, and put the mixture in a baking pan.

Beat the whites of the eggs stiff and add them, then the nuts. Set the baking pan in hot water and bake 20 minutes.

The whipped cream attends it when served.

DATE PUDDING

½ lb. of stoned dates
1 cup of cream
1 cup of bread crumbs
2 tablespoons of butter
1 cup of sugar

Clean the dates, stone them, and chop them up. Add the butter to the cream, pour it over the crumbs, and let it all soak in for several minutes. Mix in the dates and sugar well, and steam 3 or 4 hours. Serve with cream, for health and happiness.

RICE PUDDING
A LA CAMPAGNE (4 to 6 people)

½ cup of rice
½ tablespoon of butter
½ cup of sugar
1 pint of milk
2 eggs
Grated nutmeg, raisins

Cold cooked rice must soak in milk, first. For uncooked rice, boil it thoroughly and drain it; add the butter and let it cool. Add a cup of sugar and some nutmeg.

Beat up the eggs, whites and yolks separately, add them, then stir in the milk slowly, and put in the raisins. Put in a buttered baking dish and consign it to a moderate oven for an hour. Serve with preserves if you like, and cream.

RICE PUDDING A LA CANELLE

"ef yo' lay yo' min' to de Good Book, yo' fin's plen'y puzzlements; lak how-come dey mek so much talk about braid, en' don' pay no nevah-min ter rice, when it count so much mo'."

½ cup of rice
1 pint of milk
3 tablespoons of brown sugar
1 tablespoon of cinnamon

Wash the rice and mix it with the other ingredients, and put them all together, well mixed, in a baking dish. Let it cook slowly for at least 2 hours.

Give it time to cool, and serve either with preserves or cream, or both.

MARSHMALLOW CLOUD

1 pint whipping cream
2 tablespoons powdered sugar
½ lb. of chopped nuts
½ lb. marshmallows
Lady-fingers (or macaroons)
Vanilla

Whip the sugar into the cream, and add vanilla flavoring. Put in the chopped nuts and quartered marshmallows, and let the mixture stand for 2 hours. Chopped candied cherries may be added, too.

Serve in a bowl lined with lady-fingers or macaroons. Delicate and rich.

BLACKBERRY ROLL

6 cups of blackberries
Biscuit dough
Granulated sugar
Vanilla
Brandy (if possible)

Line a deep pan with biscuit dough rolled thin. Fill it with unsweetened blackberries, cover them with a layer of biscuit dough, and bake.

Serve them hot, with a hard sauce, made by beating into butter as much sugar as it will take, and adding vanilla extract or ground vanilla bean; also a tablespoon or two of brandy if possible.

This is a dish satisfying and good at any time, particularly so with a cold luncheon or supper on a summer day.

BISCUIT GLACE

"gotta watch de wedder: hot en' col' speak diff'ent ways come ter eatin'."

1 pint of whipping cream
2 eggs
½ cup of granulated sugar
1 teaspoon of vanilla
Vim and vigor

Beat the sugar well into the yolks. Whip the cream.

Mix a little of the whipped cream and add the mixture to the cream. (Without the prescribed vim and vigor the yolks go sadly to the bottom, and all is lost.) Add the vanilla and the stiffly beaten whites. Then into a mold with all of it and let it freeze at least 3 hours,— the longer, the better.

Lady fingers or macaroons may be added.

ICE BOX CAKE

"dey's de two kind o' dishes, de quick one dat won' wait: yo' hungah's got ter come to it: en' den day's de steady kin', lak cake, 'll wait fo' yo' hungah."

5 to 6 tablespoons of sugar
1 egg
⅔ tablespoon of cocoa
½ lb. (scant) of melted Nucoa Oleo
½ eggshell of milk
½ tablespoon of vanilla
Pinch of salt
Chocolate, ginger snaps (or tea-cakes)

The sugar and the whole of an egg creamed well, and the cocoa added slowly with the vanilla. Next the Nucoa Oleo heated and beaten in slowly drop by drop.

Line the cake pan with greased paper, and put in a layer of chocolate, then ginger snaps (or tea-cakes) alternating with the mixture. Place in ice box until chocolate is quite hard, then slice.

OMELET SOUFFLE

6 eggs
6 cups of powdered sugar
1 teaspoon of vanilla, salt
Beat the whites very stiff.

Cream well the sugar and 3 yolks, add the vanilla, and mix this with the whites. Put it in a cake pan and bake in a moderate oven. It is **essential** to have the eggs quite cold, and also to set the cake pan on ice before putting in the mixture.

KENTUCKY EGG NOG

6 eggs (yolks)
1 quart of cream
12 tablespoons of whiskey
6 level tablespoons of sugar

Beat the yolks and the cream briskly together,—take heart, remembering what is to come! stir in the sugar well, and lastly, certainly not leastly, add the whiskey.

ORANGE CAKE

½ lb. of powdered sugar
5 eggs (yolks)
7 eggs (whites)
2 tablespoons bread crumbs
1 orange, rind and juice
½ lb. of almonds (blanched)

Vim and vigor are essentials. Take them and beat the yolks and sugar ½ an hour. Add the orange juice and a little lemon juice, the almonds chopped extremely fine, and bread crumbs. The oven at last,—40 minutes with the oven very slow.

The pans must be those that have detachable sides. Whipping cream serves as filling and icing,—slightly sweetened and with a touch of vanilla in it.

DEVIL'S FOOD CAKE

2 cups of brown sugar
½ cup of butter
2 eggs
½ cup of buttermilk
2 cups of flour
½ cake of sweet chocolate
2 teaspoons of soda
Raisins

Beat the eggs and add the butter (not creamed). Add the butter milk with the soda in it, then flour, chocolate, and last of all raisins, and likewise chopped nuts if desired.

Caramel filling.

RAISIN CAKE

½ lb. of oleo (scant)
3 eggs
½ lb. of potato flour (or corn starch)
½ lb. of wheat flour
½ lb. of sugar
Pinch of salt
2 cups of milk
2 level teaspoons baking powder
Currants, raisins, chopped almonds
Lemon or orange flavor to taste; or
lemon peel and juice

Work the milk, eggs, and lard, into the flour. Add the sugar, then the baking powder. Orangeade or citronade or lemon peel, with some of the juice will flavor it nicely.

German origins are evident in this dish,— good ones, in any case!

BROWN BETTY

6 apples
Slices of bread
½ cup of molasses
½ cup of water
Butter, sugar, cinnamon

Toast the bread and crumble it. Peel and slice the apples. Put a layer of crumbled bread in the bottom of a baking pan; sprinkle a little sugar and cinnamon over it, and put dabs of butter about. Next, a layer of sliced apples, with the same butter, sugar, and cinnamon treatment; and so on for several layers, ending with bread crumbs. Then pour the water and molasses over it all. Set the baking dish in a pan containing water and put it in the oven for ¾ of an hour.

Almonds or raisins make a nice addition. This is a pleasant version of an old favorite.

FEATHER CAKE

4 level tablespoons of butter
1 cup of sugar
2 eggs
½ cup of flour
2½ teaspoons of baking powder
½ cup of milk
Lemon or vanilla flavoring

Cream the sugar and butter, then the eggs. Add the milk, and the flour with the baking powder in it, then fold in the whites of eggs. Flavor with lemon or vanilla. Into the oven with it, and you have an easy, inexpensive, and enjoyable cake.

PINEAPPLE UPSIDE DOWN CAKE

1 can of pineapples (small)
3 tablespoons of butter
1 cup of brown sugar
2 eggs
1 cup of sugar (granulated and a little brown)
1 cup of flour
½ cup of pineapple juice
1 teaspoon of baking powder
Vanilla or lemon extract

First, the cake pan,—prepare it by melting the butter and the brown sugar in it to cover the bottom. Strain the pineapples, cut them up, and scatter the pieces over the bottom of the pan.

Next,—a dough: Beat the eggs with the sugar, mix in the other ingredients.

Put the batter in over the brown sugar and chopped pineapple, and let it cook for ½ an hour. It melts in your mouth.

PINEAPPLE GINGER CAKE

1 cup of brown sugar
½ stick of butter
1 can of pineapple
Dough:
1¾ cups of flour
½ teaspoon of soda
1 teaspoon each of baking powder, ginger, cinnamon.
½ teaspoon each of cloves, nutmeg, and salt
3 tablespoons of shortening
½ cup of sugar
1 cup of syrup
½ cup of boiling water
1 egg

Cream the shortening and sugar, add the beaten egg, and syrup, and mix in the other ingredients. Add the water and beat well. This dough is baked in the pan prepared as above,—i. e., the brown sugar and butter are put in the cake pan and melted till they reach the boiling point. The pineapples are strained, and chopped over the melted sugar and butter.

When the dough is poured over this, let it cook for ¾ an hour.

CLABBER CAKE

¼ lb of butter
1 cup of sugar
1 egg
5 teaspoons of cocoa
1 teaspoon of soda
2 cups of flour
1 cup of clabber

Cream the butter and sugar together. Beat the egg well, and add it, then the clabber, flour, cocoa, and soda. Bake in a slow oven.

"de levee ain' gonna be mo' strong den de spot whah de crawfish is; en' dat mean ter say, yo' cake cain' be no good widout icin' de same."

CARAMEL ICING

1 lb. of brown sugar
1 cup of cream
½ cup of butter
Vanilla

Mix the ingredients together; boil 20 minutes, then beat a little and spread on cake.

MOCHA ICING

2 cups of powdered sugar
2 tablespoons of butter
2 tablespoons of cocoa
2 tablespoons of coffee
1 teaspoon of vanilla
Pinch of salt

Cream the butter and sugar and cocoa, then add the liquid and beat thoroughly. That's all,—except to put it on the cake and enjoy it.

CONDENSED MILK ICING

½ cake of unsweetened chocolate
1 can of condensed milk
1 cup of sugar
½ cup of boiling water

Put the chocolate, condensed milk and sugar in a double boiler, and when the chocolate is melted, add the water. Cook until smooth, and it is a happy touch for any cake.

SANDCOOKIES

4 eggs
½ lb. of butter
½ lb. of sugar
½ lb. of potato flour (or cornstarch)
2 scant teaspoons of baking powder
Lemon peel

Beat the butter and sugar at least ½ an hour. Then stir in the eggs, then the flour, add the lemon peel, ground fine, and the baking powder. Roll to cookie thinness and bake.

NUT BREAD

1 cup of sugar (scant)
1 cup of pecans
4 cups of flour
4 teaspoons of baking powder
1 teaspoon of salt
1 cup of milk
1 egg

Sift the flour, salt, and baking powder together, add the sugar, then the egg well beaten. Then the milk, and lastly the nuts, rolled in flour.

Give it 20 minutes to rise, then bake in a moderate oven.

OATMEAL COOKIES

1 egg (white and yolk)
½ cup of sugar
1 tablespoon of butter (melted)
1 cup of oatmeal (uncooked)
½ teaspoon of vanilla

Mix all the ingredients well together. Drop the resultant batter into a buttered pan by teaspoonfuls. Bake in a moderate oven, and be proud of the result. Your neighbor and your neighbor's children may eat and rejoice!

OATMEAL COOKIES BON ENFANT

1 cup of butter
2 cups of sugar
2 eggs
2 cups of flour
1 cup of oatmeal
1 cup of raisins (and nuts, if you will)
1 tablespoon of vinegar
2 tablespoons of baking powder
Salt

Cream the butter and sugar together. Add the eggs and the flour well sifted, then the other ingredients.

Drop the mixture by dessertspoonfuls onto a greased pan; smooth them to cookie shape, and bake in a moderate oven about ten minutes.

PECAN COOKIES

4 cups of flour
1 lb. of butter
3 cups of ground pecans
2 tablespoons of vanilla
12 tablespoons of pulverized sugar

Work the ingredients together with the hand. Shape in small crescents and bake in a moderate oven. When they are cooked and warm, roll them in some powdered sugar. The way to a man's heart!

CINNAMON ROLLS

"de preacher 'll tell yo' how a little leb'n 'll 'leb'n-up de whole o' sump'n',—well, suh, dat's how 'tis wid cinnamon."

    1 cup of cream
    ½ cup of sugar
    3 cups of flour (well sifted)
    ½ teaspoon of salt
    3 teasponos of baking powder
    Butter
    3 tablespoons of cinnamon

Mix ingredients as though for biscuit dough, but roll the resultant dough more thin.

Mix up the cinnamon and the sugar and sprinkle the mixture thickly over the dough. Pour melted butter over it all, and roll it like a jelly roll.

Slice it and lay the slices in a buttered tin. Bake 15 or 20 minutes.

Raisins and nuts may be added with the sugar and cinnamon if desired.

BROWNIES CELESTE

    1 cup of sugar
    ½ cup of butter
    ½ cup of flour
    2 eggs (yolks and whites)
    Pinch of salt
    ½ teaspoon of vanilla
    1 cup of nuts
    2 squares of chocolate

Cream the sugar and butter and beat in the eggs, flour, and salt. Then melt the chocolate, and add it to the vanilla and nuts. Mix all of this together well and pour it into a well greased pan to the depth of ½ a finger's breadth. Put the pan in a cold oven and let it cook very slowly, about ½ an hour.

The cold oven and slow cooking are important.

CRULLERS

    2 cups of sifted flour
    2 teaspoons of baking powder
    1 teaspoon of salt
    1 tablespoon of sugar
    2 level tablespoons of lard
    Ice water

Mix the ingredients, but do not handle more than necessary, and do not roll out. Use as much ice water as is necessary for the mixing. Bake 15 minutes in a hot oven.

BERTHA'S NUT COOKIES

    2 sticks of butter
    1 cup of sugar
    1 egg (yolk)
    2 cups of flour
    2 teaspoons of cinnamon
    Chopped pecans

Butter, sugar, and yolk of the egg must all be creamed together.

Mix the cinnamon with the flour and add the other mixture, stirring it together well. Work the nuts in.

Spread it thinly in a long pan greased and sprinkled with flour. Glaze with the unbeaten white of egg.

Bake in a moderate oven about 45 minutes. Cut into squares while hot, and let them cool in the pan.

Raisins may be added with the nuts.

BUTTER SCOTCH COOKIES

    2 cups of brown sugar
    1 cup of butter and lard (½ of each)
    2 eggs
    1 teaspoon of vanilla
    1 teaspoon of soda
    1 teaspoon of cream of tartar
    3½ cups of flour
    1 cut of nutmeats

Beat the sugar and eggs together; add the vanilla, then the shortening, which has been melted and cooked. Lastly the dry ingredients and nuts. The mixture is stiff enough to handle. Shape it into a loaf, put it in the ice box for at least 12 hours. Then slice it and bake it in a hot oven. You will ruin your dinner every day till they are gone, but it is worth it.

RUSSIAN ROCKS

    1 cup of butter
    1½ cups of sugar
    2½ cups of flour
    3 eggs
    1 teaspoon each of cloves, cinnamon, allspice.
    1 lb. of raisins
    1 lb. of pecans
    1 teaspoon of soda
    1 tablespoon of boiling water

Mix all the ingredients together well, the raisins and pecans last of all, except the soda, which is the final touch. It is dissolved in the boiling water before being added.

DATE TART

1 cup of dates
1 cup of nuts
1 cup of sugar
1 cup of flour
3 eggs
3 teaspoons of baking powder

Mix all the ingredients together; bake in muffin pans and serve with whipped cream.

FUDGE

2 cups of sugar
4 tablespoons of cocoa or chocolate
1 cup of milk (or pet cream)
1 tablespoon of butter
2 teaspoons of marshmallow cream
½ teaspoon of vanilla

Stir the sugar, cocoa and milk together, and let them cook over a moderate fire, till drops of the mixture harden in cold water.

Then added the melted butter, marshmallows, cream and the vanilla, beat as huskily as possible, and pour on a greased platter. Cut in squares as it cools.

"sweet in de mouf kin mean sweet in de manners, sometimes."

COCOANUT PRALINES

1 cocoanut
½ lb. of granulated sugar
½ cup of water
Cocoanut milk
A porcelain or granite pot, please

Add the water to the sugar; cook till it begins sticking to the sides of the pot. Scrape it away from the sides, add the grated cocoanut, and cook till it bubbles.

Drop from a spoon onto a marble slab, in cookie shape.

PECAN PRALINES

1 lb. of sugar
1 cup of molasses (small)
1 scant cup of water
1 lb. of pecans (weighed in the shell)

Let the sugar, water and molasses cook together on a slow fire. When they are partly cooked, add the shelled pecans, and keep the stirring in mind.

Test from time to time, on a buttered marble slab. When it is done, drop it on the slab by teaspoonfuls, so that each praline is a flat circle 3 or 4 inches in diameter.

CREOLE PECAN PRALINES

2 cups of yellow clarified sugar
4 cups of shelled pecans
¼ cup of black molasses
1 cup of boiling water

Put the sugar in a scaucepan, and add boiling water. Stir well, then place it on the stove. Add the molasses. Stir several times until the syrup forms balls in ice water.

Remove from the fire, add nuts.

Drop 2 tablespoonfuls on a marble slab, to form pralines. Remove from the slab almost at once.

CARAMEL DREAMS

3 lbs. of brown sugar
½ lb. of chocolate
2 cups of brown corn syrup
2 cups of cream
½ lb. of butter
Vanilla

Mix the ingredients and let them cook on a moderate fire an hour. Stir at intervals, with your big spoon. Then pour on a greased dish, pull off caramel size squares and wrap each separately in waxed paper.

HOT BREADS

"de bread in de oven match de spirit in de cook: ef one won' rise, de yudder won't neither."

CORN MEAL MUFFINS

2 cups of corn meal
1 cup of sour milk
1 cup of sugar
1 pinch of soda
2 tablespoons of melted lard
1 egg, 1 teaspoon of salt

Sift the meal into a bowl, and add sugar and salt. Dissolve the soda in milk and then beat it into the meal. Add an egg well beaten. Last of all, add milk and lard. Put into muffin pans well greased and hot. Bake in a quick oven.

WAFFLES

1 cup of flour
2 eggs
¼ cup of melted lard
2 teaspoons of baking powder
1 cup of milk (about)
Pinch of salt, pinch of sugar

Mix the flour, eggs and lard, add a pinch of salt and a pinch of sugar, and 2 tablespoons of baking powder. Thin with the milk, and beat vigorously.

Syrup is often used, sparingly, instead of the sugar.

WHOLE WHEAT WAFFLES

1½ cups of whole wheat flour
2 whole eggs
¼ cup of Wesson or Mazola oil
1 teaspoon of salt
1 cup of milk
2 teaspoons of baking powder

Mix the flour, eggs, and oil, add the salt, and the baking powder. Thin with the milk.

A little syrup may be added: it makes them brown prettily.

CORN BREAD

2 cups of corn meal
1 tablespoon of butter
2 eggs
1 pint of milk (or water, or ½ milk, ½ water)
1 teaspoon of baking powder
Pinch of salt

Mix the butter, and eggs together, put in the salt, cornmeal, then add the milk. Next the yeast powder. Mix it all together well.

Put it in a hot pan, not too deep, and give it 15 minutes in a hot oven.

POP-OVERS

2 eggs
1 cup of milk
5 tablespoons of flour (heaping)
Pinch of salt.

Beat the eggs separately. Add them to the milk, stir in the flour well, and add the salt. Put them in baking cups and set them in a quick oven. With a little butter and syrup, they are a treat.

FRENCH PAN-CAKES (20)

"some things sez 'anyhow' en' some say 'tek keer'; den dis-hyar pan-cake say, 'tek plen'y keer.'"

1 lb. of flour
1 egg (or 2)
Water
1 tablespoon of orange-flower water
Pinch of salt

Make a thin batter simply by stirring water into the flour, adding it very, very slowly, and stirring constantly. Add an egg; if the batter is not very thin, with that, add another. Then the orange-flower water and salt. Beat very energetically, then let it (and yourself) rest 2 or 3 hours.

Then get out a large skillet, put in enough butter to cover the bottom completely, and get it quite hot. Then drop in a spoonful of the batter, and shake the pan gently, so that the batter covers the whole bottom of the skillet. The batter should be very thin, for the ideal of a French pancake is to be as thin as paper.

Cooked on one side, it must be turned on the other. When it is done, spread a bit of butter, sprinkle it with powdered sugar, or put a little preserves on it, and roll it up like a blanket roll. Serve very hot. And your husband will never leave home.

A superb effect is to be had by putting a little brandy and sugar on the pancakes, and lighting the brandy. Better than brandy is a curacao mixture,—but where can it be had?

BATTER CAKES

1½ cups of flour
1 cup of milk
2 eggs
1 tablespoon of melted butter
1 teaspoon of baking powder

Beat the eggs separately; add them to the milk. Stir in the flour, then add the melted butter; then the baking powder. Beat well and drop by big spoonsful on the griddle. Have breakfast early, or the children will be late for school! A little syrup in the batter helps browning. A little cooked grits makes them tenderer.

HOE CAKES

1 tablespoon of flour
1 pint of sour milk
1 teaspoon of soda
Meal
Salt, syrup

Stir the flour into the milk, and then enough meal to make a good batter. Add the soda, and bake in thin cakes.

BISCUIT—(SWEET MILK)

1 quart of sifted flour
2 full teaspoons of baking powder
1 heaping tablespoon of lard
Pinch of salt
Sweet milk

Put the baking powder and salt into the flour and rub in the lard. Mix cold sweet milk with this, handling as little as possible, but mixing well till you have a soft dough.

Roll this thin, and cut with a round cutter, If you like them very thin and crisp, add a little more shortening. Roll them quite thin, and cut them about the size of a dollar. The size is a matter of taste. Put them in a griddle fitting against each other to fill it.

'BUTTERMILK' BISCUIT

1 quart of flour
1 pint of buttermilk
1 tablespoon of lard
1 scant teaspoon each of soda, salt and baking powder

Put the salt, baking powder and soda in the flour and sift it. Rub the lard into it and add the milk, to make a light dough. Cut and arange them as directed for the others.

CRUMPETS

1 quart of flour
2 tablespoons of melted butter
Milk
2 heaping spoons of baking powder
Pinch of salt

Sift the flour before measuring. Add the baking powder and salt; then the melted butter. Mix this well, then add milk gradually, enough to make a dough. Put in muffin pans, and bake in a hot oven.

BATTER BREAD

2 eggs
1½ pints of milk
1 pint of meal
1 teaspoon of melted butter (or lard)
½ teaspoon of salt

Beat the eggs very light. Pour the milk into them, and then add the meal, very deliberately, and with vigorous beating. Then stir in the salt and butter.

Have an earthen pan greased and warmed, and pour the batter in as soon as it is mixed. Bake it half an hour.

SPOON BREAD

1 pint of meal
1 pint of sour milk
1 pint of warm water
4 eggs
1 tablespoon of melted lard
Pinch of salt, 1 teaspoon of soda

Beat the eggs well. Stir the meal into the milk and water, add the eggs and salt, then the lard and soda. Bake in a greased pan.

SPOON BREAD (WITH GRITS)

Meal
Cold grits (3 tablespoons or less)
3 eggs
1 pint (or more) of milk
1 teaspoon of soda
1 tablespoon of melted lard
Pinch of salt

Beat up the eggs well. Mash the grits smooth, and mix it with the milk and eggs, adding enough meal to make a thin batter. Add the melted lard and salt and soda. Now, a greased earthen baking dish, and a good oven.

CHEESE PUFFS

½ cup (scant) of lard
1 cup of cheese (American grated)
1 cup of flour
1 teaspoon of baking powder
1 egg
Salt, pepper, cayenne

Mix thoroughly, and roll thin on slightly floured board. Cut in strips, and bake.

They lend an air,—and a taste!—to salads.

CHEESE PUFFS

½ cup of shortening
1 cup of boiling water
½ cup of pastry flour
½ cup of grated American cheese
2 eggs
Salt, cayenne

Heat the shortening and water to boiling. Turn in at one fell swoop flour, salt, and cayenne, Stir ambitiously, until the mixture clings together and more or less leaves the sides of the pan. Cheer up: this will be but a minute or two.

Beat in the cheese, and let it all cool, till the dough feels lukewarm to touch.

Drop in unbeaten eggs one at a time, beating each time till the mixture is velvety. Drop by teaspoonfuls onto an oiled baking sheet. Bake in moderate oven over 5 minutes. Trouble, but worth it.

CINNAMON TOAST

"my madam say tea-time fer talkin'; but I 'low de comp'ny lak sump'n mo'n jes' talk between dey teef."

Bread
Sugar
Cinnamon

Slice the bread very thin, and cut off the crust. Shape the slices nicely; pretty tastes as pretty looks! Melt the butter and dip the slices in. If the bread is very fresh, crisp it a little first in a moderate oven. Mix one part of cinnamon to two of sugar in a shallow dish, and the instant the toast is taken out, dip it in.

Another way: Cut the slices of bread as thick as your finger's width, then cut each slice in three strips. Fry the strips in butter; put the cinnamon and sugar mixture in a paper bag, and shake it well. It may be run back in the oven a moment if you want it quite sugared.

FRUIT TART PASTRY

A little cheese worked in the pastry to be used for fruit is a very happy touch.

CALAS TOU' CHAUD, see page 17.

PAIN PERDU, see page 18.

CAFE BRULOT

This—no longer possible, of course (?)—is a cherished old after-dinner tradition, dear to memory.

Lemon peel, thinnest outer rind
A bit of orange peel, thinnest outer rind
4 all-spice
2 cloves
8 lumps of sugar
6 parched whole coffee beans
4 aloes
1½ cups of brandy (or whiskey)
3 large cups of coffee, exceptionally strong

A silver or earthenware bowl, with a cover, capable of standing heat, were essential, and a silver ladle. The impressive thing was to bring in a great silver tray, with these utensils on it, and the other ingredients in smaller containers set about it, so that the happy guests might see the whole ritual.

Bowl and ladle were rinsed with boiling water, and then in went all the ingredients except the coffee and one sugar lump. The ladle was heated anew by a match held under it, then it dipped up a bit of the liquid from the bowl. The sugar lump was put into it, and touched with a lighted match, till it caught fire. When it blazed well it was sunk softly into the bowl, which ignited in turn. The lights in the room were put out, and the bowl blazed merrily.

Into it, slowly, was poured the coffee. It was allowed to blaze, ladled and stirred, for some moments, dramatically, the ladle dipping up the flaming contents and pouring it gently back again.

Then, when the blaze went out, or was extinguished by having the cover clapped on, the contents of the bowl was served in small coffee cups to appreciative epicures.

And so in this fading glow, Mandy and I make our departing bow, with the not ignoble hope that we have served!